# DAUGHTERS IN HIGH SCHOOL

# DAUGHTERS IN HIGH SCHOOL

## An Anthology of Their Work

EDITED BY FRIEDA SINGER

DAUGHTERS, INC.

Plainfield, Vermont

*ISBN: 0-913780-32-4*
*Library of Congress Catalog Card Number: 74-79917*

*Manufactured in the United States of America*
*Typeset by Maris Hearn*

Second Printing

POEM, Windy Wilson, p. 218, first appeared in *her-self*. Reprinted here with the gracious permission of *her-self*.

*Designed by Loretta Li*

# *Introduction*

Walk tall, daughter.
You are young, and your choices
Are as open as your brother's.
There will be no picket parades
And militant campaigns for you;
Liberation is a thing of the soul
And bears no relation to laws passed
Or battles won.
We will have succeeded only if
From our bittersweet choices,
You are born with what we fought to attain.
Daughter, I give you pride.

—from "For the Daughter I May
Someday Have" by Ellen Gray,
Tolland, Connecticut

This poem by one of the youthful contributors to this anthology expresses more succinctly than anything I could say or any literary passage from which I might quote the purpose of this anthology. When high school women students around the country were asked last spring by a new publishing house, Daughters, Inc., a publisher of books by women, to contribute manuscripts and art work to a high school anthology on any subject of their choice, including work based on their experiences as young women growing up in contemporary American society, neither the publishers nor the editor of this anthology could anticipate the results.

Those acquainted with the excellent junior and senior high school anthologies published by Scholastic Book Services, *Peppermint* (1960) and *Bittersweet* (1968), which are based on the best selections from scholastic writing awards contests for the past twenty to forty years, realize that literary talent is expressed at an extremely early age—and the judges of these contests, professional writers of stature, have year after year remarked on the sensitivity and rare imagination of the contestants. Jerome Brondfield, the editor of *Bittersweet*, a senior high school anthology, in seeking a generalization that can be significant in the creative thinking of teen-age writers, claims it is "a noticeable preoccupation with death and the bittersweet sensitivity felt in the process of growing up." "Humor, tragedy, action, reflection, love, hate, beauty, ugliness—you will find all these in *Peppermint*," claims David A. Sohn, the editor of *Peppermint*, a Junior high school anthology.

Strongly contrasting with the aforementioned, highly publicized, highly competitive anthologies based on prize-winning selections culled from thousands of nation-wide contributions, are a number of new publications edited or compiled by teacher-writers conducting experimental classes in writing either within or outside the conventional school environment. Stressing the non-competitive aspects of writing, these teacher-writers have encouraged their students to "tell it like it is," urging them to break free from the constraints of form or mechanics. One of the most popular of these anthologies, *The Me Nobody Knows: Children's Voices from the Ghetto* (1969) served as source material for a popular Broadway musical-drama. Based on the writing of two hundred primary and secondary school children, ranging from seven to eighteen years of age, most of them Black or Puerto Rican, the editor Stephen M. Joseph's intention was to diminish the stigma of the word "ghetto" by showing that its inhabitants if given "an open climate to write, have a tremendous amount to say and are anxious to speak . . ." The subject matter of

*The Me Nobody Knows* reflects the realities of growing up poor in an urban area, of seeing the outside world mostly as a fantasy and of wondering about the things one cannot see or touch.

Whereas the aforementioned anthologies stress *either* 1) creative excellence on the basis of specific criteria and the critical evaluation of a panel of literary judges *or* 2) the responses of a selected segment of the population on a given theme, this anthology is concerned *both* with creative excellence *and* the responses of a selected segment of the population on a given theme—mainly the realities of growing up female in American society today. The contributors to this anthology did not number in the thousands; nor was material selected as a result of a series of preliminary literary try-outs and eliminatory contests. No prizes were awarded to the "best" literary manuscripts, no special criteria as to length, literary excellence or recommendation by a faculty member were established. (Nevertheless, many faculty members throughout the nation were kind enough to encourage their students to submit material.)

The quality of the contributions to this anthology, solicited only through a brief notice in selected newspapers and periodicals throughout the nation, was so uniformly excellent that it was difficult to select those most appropriate for publication. A number of the short stories and novellas submitted by youthful contributors, several only thirteen years of age, ran from fifty to one hundred and fifty pages long and revealed a high degree of talent, ingenuity and ambition. These precocious young writers deserve and will undoubtedly be given an audience in the future.

Limitation of space made it impossible to consider for acceptance lengthy contributions where considerable cutting and editing were necessary. Where a number of submissions were similar in theme or form, the most original or succinct were selected. Mainly, the criteria for selection of material were literary excellence, originality of theme and form and a sense of honesty, urgency and commitment to the subject matter. Our goal, also, was to represent the many concerns of American women in high school and to represent as many sections in the nation as possible. The anthology is not a definitive one but a first of its kind, and we hope a beginning.

"Daughter, I give you pride," says Ellen Gray, of Tolland, Connecticut. This is a major purpose of this collection of writing and art work by high school women in the year 1973. In 1929, the English novelist, Virginia Woolf in *A Room of Her Own* speculated on the sad state of Shakespeare's alleged sister Judith, "She died young—alas, she never wrote a word . . ." To Virginia Woolf, it was impossible for a woman, what with the economic, social, political and psychological restrictions placed upon women at that time, to have written the plays of Shakespeare *in the age of Shakespeare.* However, it was Woolf's belief "that the poet who was Shakespeare's sister lives in you and me, and in many other women who are not here tonight, for they are washing up the dishes and putting the children to bed." To Virginia Woolf, Shakespeare's sister needed, like all poets, *only the opportunity* to walk among us in the flesh. This would come about if we worked for her—and "that so to work, even in poverty and obscurity, is worthwhile." The purpose of this anthology is to provide a place and, we hope, an opportunity so that "the dead poet who was Shakespeare's sister will put on the body which she has so often laid down."

> Women
> about women
> for women
> is after all
> just people

says Laura Gordon of Rolling Hills Estates California, another contributor to this anthology. How concise an expression of what women's collective unconscious has communicated to her from prehistory to the present!

In 1792, Mary Wollstonecraft in her historic work, *A Vindication of the Rights of Women*, criticized the books of instruction written by men of genius in her day as viewing women as subordinate beings, and not as a part of the human species ". . . and, who can tell, how many generations may be necessary to give vigour to the virtue and talents of the freed posterity of abject slaves?" In 1953, Simone de Beauvoir in her chapter, "The Woman in Love," in *The Second Sex* confirms woman's subordinate position: "There is no way out for her than to lose herself, body and soul, in him who is represented to her as the absolute, as the essential . . . . she will humble herself to nothingness before him. Love becomes for her a religion." In fall, 1973, during an interview with Dorothy Tennov, recorded in the February/March, 1974, issue of *Prime Time*, Simone de Beauvoir, in responding to what men fear most about feminism today, claimed, "They fear competition in their work outside the home, and they fear not having a servant at home . . . . Mostly, I guess, it's the fear of not having a servant at home . . . Men will accept a woman working outside if she continues to do exactly the same work for them at home."

"I ask no favors for my sex—I surrender not our claim to equality—All I ask of our brethren is that they take their feet from off our necks, and permit us to stand upright on the ground which God has designed us to occupy," said Sarah Grimke, pioneer feminist in *The Equality of the Sexes and the Conditions of Women* in 1838. The high school women contributors to this anthology may or may not be familiar with the work of Mary Wollstonecraft, Sîmone de Beauvoir or Sarah Grimke, but the foregoing sentiments are echoed in their poetry, essays and short stories.

The high school women contributors to this anthology may or may not be familiar with the suit brought by New York City high school women in 1969 against the Board of Education to be admitted to Stuyvesant High School, an all-male specialized, academic high school, but the need for equal educational, intellectual and cultural opportunities for both men and women is echoed in the writing of contributors to this anthology. My afternoon newspaper, *The New York Post* of January 25, 1974, reports that a federal court judge has ruled that 24 male applicants be allowed to take the Hunter High School entrance exam along with some 3,000 females. Hunter High School, a prestigious academic high school, has heretofore been restricted to young women. Surely elimination of discrimination in public institutions can prove beneficial to both sexes!

"When I first moved to N.Y. from Virginia, I wanted to join a handball team. After I started playing better than the fellows did, I was kicked off the team."

"When I was small, I used to handwrestle but my mother told me this would give me muscles. You're left with the housework while your brother prepares for his life's work."

"I don't think a man will fully accept a woman wanting to be herself; partially but not fully."

These are three approximate quotations from a consciousness-raising session conducted at Columbia University's annual Scholastic Press Association's convention on March 16, 1973 for high school women interested in learning about, speaking out and writing on women's issues. The purpose of this session, attended by over two hundred fifty high school women, staff members and editors of their high school newspapers and literary magazines, was to introduce high school women journalists to the women's movement, to conduct a consciousness-raising session on the subject of conventional male and female role-playing, and to encourage the participants to contribute material to this anthology. The high school women contributors to this anthology may or may not have attended the aforementioned session at Columbia University last March, but their sentiments on breaking out of conventional sex roles, one of the most comprehensive sections of this anthology, echo those expressed at this conference.

The concerns of high school women in rural New England, in Appalachia, in Southern California, and in the industrial cities of the Midwest and the Northeast are surprisingly similar. High school women are not concerned solely with local color or with local custom; with traveling to the moon; with tales of space travel or science fiction; they do not write of physical combat, competition on the football field or the tennis court, or of risk-taking escapades.*

What high school women do write about are what William Faulkner in his "Nobel Price Acceptance Speech" described as "*problems of the human heart in conflict with itself* which alone can make good writing because only that is worth writing about, worth the agony and the sweat." Faulkner believed that the writer's voice need not merely be the record of humanity but one of the pillars to help us *endure and prevail.* The young women contributors to this anthology are strongly aware of the fact that in six seconds "a seed can start to grow, a life can expire." They are aware of the fragility of life, and reaching out for what is yet to be born, they search for those resources within themselves, physical, intellectual, emotional and spiritual, which will enable them to survive and to endure.**

This anthology is divided into six parts. Each one expresses a strong concern of the contributors and includes representative poetry, essays or short stories. In the first part, "The Unknown," high school women confront the mysterious and un-

*Among the excellent novellas which we could not publish because of their great length, however, were a number of suspenseful and ingenious detective and mystery tales in which a female protagonist either outwits or is at least the equal of her male partner, and a few heart-warming tales of family deprivation and survival in the face of enormous odds.

**That high school journalists throughout the country have become increasingly involved in feminism, and increasingly active in effecting social change in their communities was evidenced at the 1974 Columbia Scholastic Press Association's annual convention in a seminar on "Search for Self: Feminism in the High School." Among the areas in which young journalists are effecting change are in organizing workshops in consciousness-raising, in human identity, in feminist literature and history; in creating new non-sexist textbooks; and in campaigning for new patterns of non-sexist behavior and life-styles.

known in their environment with bewilderment and courage. The poetry in this part ranges from reactions to growing up, encountering new faces and new experiences, whether in a theater or in school, to a more sophisticated questioning of the evil in the universe. Included are poems on war ("Across the dreamy autumn sky/cuts a stark white line of poison gas"), death and destruction ("and the world blows up,/will we have time to say 'I'm sorry' "), as well as poems on the ambiguities of death in life, evil in good ("Thorns among the soft grapes; flowers and wine.") and the desert in the mind.

Whereas a humorous essay in this part reflects on the ambiguity of applying a college education to solving household chores, the more serious essays deal with death in the family and the subject of mastectomy. The stories concentrate also on the bewilderment of growing up female and the psychological deaths, self-ravagements and rebirths one endures and survives.

In the second part, "Roles," high school women see themselves playing different roles with various people in an effort to find out "Am I normal?" or "Am I real, real, real?" In the poetry in this part, high school women see themselves as a reflection of the world around them ("I realize that sometimes/I have to hear other people's words/To realize what I feel"), a part of everything they experience, or as a walking oddity, hiding behind walls, hoping no one will see. (It is not a blessing to be able to turn and say, 'This is me.' ") In their essays, high school women question their roles as teenagers or as young women "who wake up screaming out of dreams." In their stories, high school women identify with Joshua, a crow, a beloved but imprisoned creature seeking freedom, or with Tinky, the cat, whose extra-sensory perception, even in its death throes, reveals exceptional empathy and self-sacrifice.

In the third part, "The Male Protagonist," high school women transcend the confines of their immediate environment in order to assume a male voice and identify with the tension, the violence, the physical and moral concerns of the masculine world. As most of the poems included in this anthology are lyrical and personal in theme and voice rather than dramatic or narrative, no poetry is included in this section. However, the essays in this part deal with the realities of death and violence as well as the moral courage of a Vietnam veteran, twenty-six years old, confronting a school board that orders his suspension. The short stories in this part deal with loners who refuse to give up in the face of poverty, the pollution in the environment or death in the Sierra Mountains.

In the fourth part, "Questioning," high school women confront the purpose of the universe and their roles in it. ("Galaxies of eternal truths waltz/ in their predetermined elliptical orbits./There is no escape/from the known," claims Dianne-Marie Piche of Hicksville, New York in "Inertia.") The poetry in this part reflects on whether life is a series of existential questions, freeze-dried Kharma, a chess game, a waiting for the crucifixion, a charade or self-mastery. Certainly these are questions that might have been asked by Donne, Blake, Yeats, Dickinson, or Frost! The essays in this part similarly question the purpose of the human condition, recognizing that survival depends on acceptance of this condition whether one lives in

Appalachia, Verdun or California. The stories in this part overlap those in Part Three.

In the fifth part, "Relationships," young women seek fulfillment through their involvement with others. ("Leave a token of yourself for others/À look, a gesture, a thought/Let it bloom in the world," says Susee Radke of Omaha, Nebraska.) In the poetry in this part, young women eschew isolation in wooden boxes in order to develop their natural talents, their empathy and friendship, as well as their skills for bridging the generation gap and overcoming their conflicts with the opposite sex. However, for many young women the sexual conflict remains unresolved. Whereas for Heidi Libner (Michigan), "A custom made slot appears/and you are filed/into/me," for Reiko Obata (California), "Love affects me very little anymore/I used to live for love," and for Kathie Merrill (Vermont), "You lose, you would-be manfatherhusband." Whereas the essays in this part cast an amused eye upon the joys and tribulations of family life, the eye is jaundiced when it surveys the break-up of teen-age romances. Similarly, short stories in this part contrast the growth of a friendship between two young women of different racial backgrounds with the break-up of a high-school romance.

In the sixth part, "Walk Tall, Daughter," young women actively question their preordained roles as goddesses or sex objects and the male roles of protectors and law-givers, and they seek new relationships between the sexes based on equality. In the poetry section, young women speak with a vigor and a strength of the tensions of growing up female ("I used to be quiet/People even called me shy/Maybe because I held it all in too many years"), of living on pedestals ("The airissotight/I can no longer breathe"), of living the acquiescent, inactive life whereas the male is taught to be aggressive and brutal. Between the two sexes in an unequal relationship only tension exists ("Little does he realize/gods will die, too."). Until masculine arrogance is curbed and feminine pride is restored "maybe it's better to separate/instead of spending our energies/on trying/to become one (won),"says Windy Wilson of Ann Arbor, Michigan.

In the essays in this part, high school women reveal skillful irony and wit in an appraisal of the multifold restrictions of growing up Asian-American or in the performance of typical puberty rites, such as the purchase of sanitary napkins. Clever satire appears in this section in two imaginative, futuristic fantasies of an oppressive matriarchal society. In the short stories in this final part, a high degree of skill and sophistication is revealed in a retelling of six familiar fairy tales or in the dilemma of an unmarried school teacher who "wasn't odd or weird anymore, just different" in her espousal of the single state. Stories dealing with marriage reveal the hazards of trying to educate an unliberated mate and the risks of attempting to reform an incompatible one.

This anthology is not intended as a finally definitive statement of high school women throughout the nation. Rather, it is a sample of a variety of students from wholly different parts of the country and of the culture. Some selections are highly sophisticated and technically skillful, others are unpretentious and unadorned. We can conclude, however, from these selections that young women growing up female in America today are more alike than unlike; that they write with an urgency and an honesty of purpose of the deepest concerns of the human spirit; that they care about gaining a consciousness about themselves as members of a society they can learn to change.

*Frieda Singer*

# *Acknowledgments*

First, thanks go to the many sincere and talented contributors to this volume, to those whose work was included at the present time. We wish you the best of luck with your writing career. Then, we wish to thank the many teachers throughout the country, many of whom did not identify themselves, but who were kind enough to encourage their students to contribute material to this volume.

The editor is deeply grateful to the Publishers, June Arnold and Parke Bowman, who conceived of this unique anthology and whose gentle sisterly prodding and expert editorial advice and assistance made it possible. She is also deeply appreciative for the enthusiasm and encouragement of Charles R. O'Malley, Director of Columbia Scholastic Press Association, who arranged two seminars on feminism during the Columbia Scholastic Press Association's annual conventions in 1973 and 1974.

Next, thanks go to Rickie Flanders, assistant editor of *New York Teacher*, the official publication of the New York State United Teachers, for extensive news coverage which gained us excellent publicity and many fine contributions. We are also grateful for the moral support of the supervisors and teachers at Central Commercial High School, New York, New York, especially Simpson Sasserath, principal, Charles G. Spiegler, Language Arts Supervisor, Patricia Seabrook, assistant principal, and Liz Masters, who served as my student teacher during the Spring 1973 semester.

Finally, many thanks go to the student editors of *Transition*, the literary magazine at Central

Commercial High School for their outstanding creative efforts as pioneers in the area of feminism from 1968 to the present date; Deborah Singletary, Alley Del Rio, Bernarde Edwards, Kevin Sweetser, Gus Steffan, Arlene Fraas, Gloria Bass and Kim Joseph. And a special thank you to Lydia Sims and to Laurence Sims for help in typing, editing, and for many sound suggestions.

# Contents

## PART II/Roles

## PART III/The Male Protagonist



## PART IV/Questioning

## PART V/Relationships

## PART VI/Walk Tall, Daughter

## ARTWORK

# The Unknown

## PART I

*Nettie Spiwack*
*New York, New York*

# WE HAVE LEARNED

We have learned
that the past dies with
each step forward we take.
Sometimes we lie
dormant in the present
dwelling on what we are missing
and what has died,
when we should be
reaching out to what
is yet to be born.

*Lois Douglass*
*Scarborough, Maine*

# FACES

Faces through hot tea and talk mist,
shadowed blues and mustards and greys
playing peripheral games around our table;
in this dappled way
our eyes gently met;
and the moment to moment surprise of life
has been illuminated beyond each day.

*Tacy Bowlin*
*Schenectady, New York*

# CHILDHOOD

I wanted to hold it—
hug it tightly
but they were around and i was afraid
so i picked it up
and ran with it hidden
underneath my shirt
closed the door
and on my bed
carefully took it out—
so limp in my hands—
i brushed the dust off
took my childhood into my hands,and wept.

*Lynn Stein*
*Queens, New York*

# ON THIS SIDE

All the past is lived
in dreams of each spring
when the mountains grow again.
This seventeenth year
has been no different
in passing too quickly.

The brilliant sadness of this fleeting rebirth
reaches up through the deepening sky
persuading me to drink
another round of wine,
uniting my sorrow
with that of the jaded leaves
crumbling too soon.

Above me
birds fly towards the north
unconcerned
over the changing images
below them.
They somehow know
just where they are heading.

*Penny Oliphant*
*Portland, Maine*

## SIX SECONDS

Six Seconds
    Believe it or not
It's a long period of time
A jet can fly a whole mile
A baby can open its eyes
A seed can start to grow
A life can expire.

*Carla Abel*
*Huntington, New York*

## THE CACTUS

We will never taste a drop
    of the sweet nectar of peace
        on
            our
                parched
                    throats.
    Until,
we are injured, calloused and torn
    by its sharp needles
        And then
            we
                find
                    it.
        Lying there,
in the middle of it all.

*Pamela Anderson*
*Huntington, New York*

## FRENCH ROSE

Figures float, bobbing water-line cork pieces—
Accidental swirls and ripples splash the bottle sides,
Mocking the grapes whose wrath manifests
    its boundaries in the depths of the wine.

Tributes form in the ever-larger muddled circles
As the bits of cork fall to the outline of the roses
Envisioned intertwined with the twisting stalks
    of vines sun-browned and dried—

Thorns among the soft grapes;
Flowers and wine.

*Laurel E. Fitch*
*Syracuse, New York*

# YOU DON'T HAVE TO BE TOLD TO KNOW

My back leaning against one armrest and my legs resting on the other, I am sitting comfortably on the chair in the living room. The picture window behind me displays, from four stories up, a typical day in early January. It is calm outside, but it must be bitter cold. From my vantage point, I can see the cars in the driveway and the surrounding red brick, six story apartment buildings. A blanket of whiteness covers everything but the smallest patch of ominous gray in the sky.

Angelina, our cleaning woman, is sitting on the couch in the adjoining room watching television. Canned laughter, can of beer in her hands, she is laughing at something that is not funny. I look at her but she does not see me. We are in different worlds.

My thoughts wander to the morning, a few hours earlier, when my parents had awakened me in an unusual manner. It was Saturday, and on Saturdays, I was accustomed to sleeping late as I didn't have to go to school. But this morning, I was awakened quite early by the sound of my mother's voice telling me that she and my father were going to my grandparents' house and wouldn't be late. A bit puzzled but too tired and groggy to think about it very much, I went back to sleep.

But, now, as I sit gazing out the window I can not escape the feeling anymore. Something is not quite right and it can be sensed throughout the house. I look at the canvas on the wall that my grandfather painted and it seems to leer back at me. The entire room seems as if it is laughing at me and for no real reason. But, somehow, I feel strangely serene and detached.

I watch the sky grow gray as the day progresses. Perhaps it is going to storm. It has been hours since I have spoken to my parents, but it seems like days. My stomach is beginning to play games with me and I am tired of sitting. I need some reason to leave this chair but I just can not think of any. Why is that damn painting still looking at me?

Thoughts of my grandfather enter my mind and soon I cannot think of anything else. All the good times we had—all the brilliant things he had done. He used to take me into his studio in the cellar and show me his unfinished paintings. He would tell me what he planned to paint and then show me how he would do it. His accomplishments in life had been great and varied. At one time he invented a ball point pen but he never bothered to have it patented, thinking it wouldn't sell. He attended Cooper Union College, but he never bothered to graduate because he was a Jew. At that time there was no place in engineering for a Jew. Few even got as far as he did. In his lifetime he had been an artist, an inventor, an engineer, an interior decorator, a carpenter, and a factory-worker. Oh, Papa David . . . . The ringing of the telephone brings me back to my senses and I slowly get up to answer it.

"Hello. This is Aunt Birdie. When is the funeral?"

I told her that I didn't know and I slowly, quietly, and calmly hung up the phone. Her question merely confirmed what I had known intuitively all along.

*Debbie Kameros*
*New York, New York*

# ECLIPSE

It was almost time. A crowd gathered gradually on the dry, baked beach. The noon sun blazed, broiling the onlookers as a smaller sphere crept slowly toward it. Where the beach had stretched itself to meet a miscellany of hotels, a lone figure stumbled to join the crowd. When Esme finally recognized the pale, tanless figure in the black mallot, she pulled herself from her mother's side and ran to greet her. She wouldn't have run normally (Mother didn't like her to run), but she hadn't seen Danielle for two days.

Danielle stopped, then squinted with her hand shading her eyes, up at the sun and its sabatour. Esme stood breathless waiting to be taken notice of. She knew what was coming, that teacher smile and the pat on the head. If she endured this bit of Danielle which she didn't like, then another Danielle would show herself soon.

"Esme, you've come to watch the eclipse," Danielle said as she bent down, messing the small child's long, dark hair with the pat of her hand.

"You've forgotten your cellophane sheets. Mother says you can't look at an eclipse without cellophane sheets," Esme said.

Danielle started in the direction of the crowd again saying, "Well, I suppose I won't look then," as she lifted her thick black hair off her back and tied it up loosely.

She had been crying, Esme could tell by the red, spotty color of her face. Esme would share her cellophane with Danielle. Both were silent until they contacted the other sweating, expectant spectators.

Esme spoke, "You have not been on the beach lately. You haven't been here for two days. I waited."

Adjusting herself in the sand Danielle said, "I sat in my hotel room thinking, 'I must meet Esme today;' however, urgent business, of the utmost importance, kept me from our rendezvous. Only urgent business could keep me away from our daily swim."

Esme plopped herself in the sand by Danielle and was momentarily content. A nervous, disapproving, sidelong glance from her mother prodded her into further conversation though, "Mother says you are accentric. What's 'eccentric'?"

"Eccentric," Danielle considered thoughtfully, "is coming to watch an eclipse without cellophane sheets."

"Are you an artist?" Esme pushed onward.

Danielle looked out into the blurred, blue of the ocean reflectively, "Now, Esme, I'm not so sure of that. I was two years ago, but now I am not sure. If art is not seen, is there art?"

Esme ignored the question. "Mother says you were lucky and that now your past is catching up with you."

"Oh yes, it's catching up. I'm stuck here unprotected, without a lotus tree," Danielle said. "Actually, I'm expecting it any minute."

All raised their ludicrous colored sheets of cellophane to gawk at the battle between the lucidity of the sun and the sordid moon. All knew the outcome, the victor. Within minutes the crowd had dispersed; the drama was over. They each ran for separate shelters from the sun's heat.

Esme remained with danielle, deaf to her mother's calls. Danielle walked gracelessly, though not awkwardly, to the edge of the water with Esme at her side. They debated on whether or not to enter the water.

"Esme," Danielle said as a wave teased their feet, "what would you do if the moon never uncovered the sun; if it were always dark?"

"I don't know, maybe go live on the moon where it would be light. What would you do?" Esme asked.

"I don't know; maybe go live on the moon with you." She looked down at Esme, "Having had light so long, being in the dark constantly just wouldn't be right."

Esme was growing tired. Danielle was uneasy. A swim was definitely out of the question, vetoed by their unanimous decision against it. Galloping all the way, Danielle carried Esme back to the hotel where her mother waited. They parted with the click of the elevator door, the floor of which was very sandy.

Esme shuffled out on the third floor, a yawning for a farewell. Danielle rode the elevator to the roof of the hotel, the seventh floor where, after little hesitation, she leaped to her death.

*Mary Yeager*
*Indianapolis, Indiana*

## INTRUDERS

Across the dreamy autumn sky,
cuts a stark white line of poison gas,
flowing from airborne engines.
And the whispery fingers of the sun-streaked clouds
reach out to us—
begging—
pleading—
to paint the sky the colors of the rainbow—
without intrusion.

*Rona Milch*
*East Northport, New York*

## NIGHTMARE AVENUE

Matinal screams etch themselves
into window panes;
Sandpaper words scratch the walls,
yearning for a dawning light—
a release from madness.
Gnarled hands try to touch
something real as
they flick all the bad dreams
from their fingertips.

*Cille Koch*
*Port Washington, New York*

## REFLECTIONS

when the sea dries up
and the sun turns cold
will we have time to
  say good-bye?

when the bomb is dropped
and the world blows up
will we have time to
  say i'm sorry?

*Emily Carla Blum*
*New York, New York*

## LOSS

for S/Sgt John Young, P.O.W. of Viet Nam

I've always thought:
  IF WE'RE GOING TO
  FIGHT A *WAR* . . .
  *WIN* IT!

    but *war* is death.

And how can you *win*
    if you're

            dead?

*Deborah A. Spivey*
*Wood Dale, Illinois*

# ORCHESTRA SEAT

There is a time, just before the house lights dim
People talking and waving to all
They've seen before.
A hum of voices and of laughter.
Everyone has found their place, and friends,
A portrait of contentment, middle age.

The lights go down
    Everything stills
And just before the scene begins
A moment of absolute dark—
Gripping, maybe terrifying.

And in that dark
No matter how close the friends you came in with
    You're alone
No touch of hand can bridge that dark;
And after a free-form moment
The stage lights come up
And you're caught watching a new scene.

*Laurie Walker*
*Syracuse, New York*

# THE MAGICIAN

The magician
Up
Placidly
Sets
His equipment
Before his audience,
His black hazy eyes
Peering out—
Shadowing His
Plastered warts and
Papier-mâché nose

And he
Smiles . . .
Gold teeth
Protruding from his
Red rubbery Lips
And
He waves his
Magic wand
Over all that is
Indifferent
To his cardboard hat . . .

And
He reaches
In
For what he hopes will be
A rabbit . . .
Complete with
Cotton tail . . .

And his hand
Sinks
Farther
Down
Into a fathomless eternity
Of unanswered
Questions.
Down
Down
Down
Down
Into his
Failure,
The man
Turned in shame toward the
Nearest

EXIT.

*Laura Stein*
*Great Neck, New York*

# "PLEASE GOD, DON'T LET MOMMY DIE"

"Please God, don't let mommy die."

I repeated those words again and again, until they became a chant, numbing my mind to peace. Although they came to me two years ago, I still repeat them desperately hoping to hear a voice reassuring me that there is no need for fear. But the fear of my mother's death will never leave me, just as the fear of cancer will never leave my mother.

I didn't sense anything unusual, as I walked home from the bus, early in November of 1970. My mother had told me she was going to the hospital for a test, but I expected her to be home by three o'clock. As I walked into the house, I heard my father talking on the phone. He hung up when he realized that I was home.

"Hi Kathy, how was school?"

"It was okay. Did you have a good golf game?"

"I didn't play golf today."

"Oh."

I wasn't listening to him, as I am in the habit of doing. Although I answered his questions, my thoughts were elsewhere. Suddenly the tears in his eyes, the arms hugging me protectively, and the sobbing in between his words, reached my brain. At first I heard only fragments of his sentences. They contained new words that sounded as horrible as the actions and things they described . . . . cancer, malignant, and mastectomy. I made no reply but waited for my mind to accept their meaning. We stood in the middle of the room, clinging to each other, our faces and hair wet from our tears. My books and papers had fallen to the floor and lay scattered about my feet. They acted like a barrier and for a few minutes we were protected from the sorrow and agony that would fill our lives.

My mother came home in a few weeks. We suffered with her as her mind and body slowly healed. I gritted my teeth each time she exercised, trying to reach her arms a little higher than the day before.

My dream world was shattered by the suffering of those two years. I realized there were things more important than material possessions. I could enjoy a walk on the beach with my parents more than I had enjoyed shopping for new clothes. The expensive clothes that my friends paraded in no longer made me sulk with jealousy. Good health became my most treasured possession.

I also treasured life more. One values every minute after death has come so close. It is hard to forget old habits, and there are times when I feel envious. But the image of a young girl sitting alone in the dark whispering, "Please God, don't let mommy die" kills those feelings.

*Kathy Fontwit*
*Palos Verdes, California*

# VIGNETTE

The sterile morgue echoed every footstep, whisper, and tear; each resounded in shock and grief. The mechanical, apathetic attendant uncovered the body of a young brunette, a bluish tint from the drowning replacing the former rosy cheeks.

"Yes, that is Vicky," her mother said, turning quickly so as not to shatter her fragile egg of agony.

A policeman, supporting her quaking body, said, matter-of-factly, "We're looking into every possibility . . ." A questioning face looked up at him.

"But there is a strong possibility of suicide. No bruises, no sign of struggle, no—" Collapsing into the stranger's arms, she screamed hysterically.

Before the telephone call summoning her to the hospital several hours ago, Vicky's mother had entered slowly into her daughter's room. The ominous breath of anxious uncertainty whispered its heavy presence into this neat, yet tacky room whose usual anonymity knelt to the strange newcomer. Its seventeen-year-old inhabitant's paraphernalia of school letters, cheerleader's jacket, rock posters, records, school books, and the like were sleeping in coerced stiffness as if to imitate their owner.

Struggling with the forbidding presence she sensed in the room—she pondered what might have happened to Vicky. Where could she be at two in the morning when she had just intended to have some fun with girl friends at a football game? Perhaps 20 percent of her healthy good looks and 80 percent of her gullible conviction that people are honest were ingredients mixed in a bowl of circumstances. What could emerge from this recipe? Fantasies of accidents frolicked frantically across the woman's screen mind but were quickly cremated in an oven of logic.

What could a person want with Vicky? Though she was attractive, it was in a stereotyped "cute" way, and Vicky never excelled in her despised school work. She preferred helpful and helping girl friends, and once a private kiss in her lonely night, to the parental discipline she detested. Still, she was seemingly perpetually smiling and giggling and quite happy. And never had she returned home, not once, late!

Her entire life's legacy was written in a page of her diary, the only page left after the others had purposely been burned. Her mother was rummaging searchingly through Vicky's room for a picture of her friend when she discovered the small journal several days after the funeral. She read the scratched-out lines, looked away for a moment, quietly closed the book, and continued busily looking for a picture.

"Is this all I am—a piece of play-dough I have chosen to portray in the hands of teachers, parents, and laws—my gods? If this is all, I want no part in it. And this is all . . ."

*Wendy Molyneaux*
*Middleport, New York*

## EATING IS

eating is . . .
hot chocolate that scorches the
tip of
your
tongue, but warms
your numb
nose
with a milky mocca mustache
impudent
peas playing
hide and go
seek

or
a
frolicking tag with a
frustrated
fork.
hippopotomus HERO
sandwiches
open
your mouth W
I
D
E
but
beware that the
insides
do
not
fall
out.

frothy fruit fillings
in
dignified fruit pies
peeping
out curiously from
beneath
the
crust
oooooooooozzzing
out
all
over my fingers
just
so they can
go on a
trip to the
bathroom.

*Jessica Teich*
*Huntington, New York*

# LEARNING IS

President Nixon flies to China.
Children die from falling napalm.
Prisoners of war return from Vietnam.
The bugging at Watergate becomes a major political
issue.
And I sit in a schoolroom and learn about them.

In Latin, -*ae* is the feminine nominative, plural ending.
Running is an English verb, active voice.
. . . These two points are colinear.
$SO_4$ is a radical in chemistry.
And I sit in a schoolroom and learn about them.

Some men are just plain crazy, according to my
psych teacher.
ATP is adenine triphosphate.
Tres means three in Spanish.
Man is a member of the primates.
And I sit in a schoolroom and learn about them.

Why . . . . ?

I LOVE IT!!!!!

*Joelle Perseille*
*Hollis, Maine*

# EMPTINESS IS

Flaming July suns
have glared
upon the burning sand carcasses.
The wind is a cracked, pierced whistle
twirling its magic wand
and
transforming the chained sand
into swirling, madman pinwheels
hurling the myriad crystals
across the naked spaces
of a cinnamon inferno
blinding the sun by its own tornado.
The desert of mind also blinds;
a barren void
it possesses no emerald oasis
and the truth mirage.

*Cheryll Galvin*
*Omaha, Nebraska*

## WINTER IS

Sharp
and cruel
threatening to end
the days of laughter
to freeze the smiles in
a fixed position to
restrict a leaf
from falling
winter

*Cille Koch*
*Port Washington, New York*

## AUTUMN IS

Autumn is a fire of orange and red;
Glowing to keep us warm and safe,
Until winter comes to sting us
With his cold.

Autumn is a crying heart;
I can't see the tears,
But I feel the pain that comes
Each time the wind blows,
And I don't know why.

Autumn is an old man;
He still has life,
But he knows death is coming,
And he lets go, just as I do,
When I feel Autumn.

*Karen Sue Fiegl*
*Canisteo, New York*

# A MIGHTY RIVER

And I was part of a mighty river,
Rushing, crashing,
And the rest of the river was made up of the people
I knew,
Never stopping, always searching;
I was they, and they were me, and together we were
a river.
Rushing, crashing,
Then one day we narrowed though still speeding,
And sailed over a peaceful brook,
Trees and flowers, beauty and wonder,
And as we passed, I saw that I knew these people too;
They called to us, and I slowed down to listen.
What they said was right and real;
I wanted to have what they had, and I shouted to them;
They reached out their arms, and I struggled back and
grasped their hands.
Then I looked at the others passing,
Rushing, crashing,
And it was my choice.
That day I let go of the only warmth I had ever touched,
And went on with the others, searching,
Rushing, crashing,
Only to find at the end, an ocean,
Big, empty!
And suddenly I was alone

sinking, sinking . . . . . .
deeper, deeper . . . . . .
colder, colder . . . . . . .

*Karen Sue Fiegl*
*Canisteo, New York*

# FOUR YEARS IN HIGH SCHOOL—FOUR YEARS IN COLLEGE

Ah, morning again. As they said in my earth science class, when spring is approaching, each day the sun rises earlier. It's already time to go wake the kids for school. Anthropology, yes, I do believe it was anthropology where I learned that it was a natural thing for people to sleep. "Come on kids. Time to get up. It's morning. Good morning." Next I get the breadwinner up. I can still remember the first time we met. It was in high school during an Algebra II class. We were doing problems like: $(1+\sec\Theta)\ (\sec\Theta 1)\ \frac{\sin\Theta\ \sec\Theta}{\cos\Theta\ \sec\Theta}$. That class has done so much for me. Oh, here I am wasting my time thinking about such silly things, when I have to get breakfast. Now, let's see, the directions say that you should boil water with salt in it. Yes, and if you add enough salt it'll supersaturate. Just as in Chemistry.

Oh thank God, the kids are off to school. Just enough time to write a letter before the mail comes. I musn't forget to use those techniques from expository writing class like fantastic realities and words that speak to each other and all those connotations should be just right.

Let's see . . . should I say . . . there! Lick the stamp and it's ready to go. Oh those kids! That living room is as filthy as ever. I'll have to vacuum the rug again today. Look at that dirt get sucked up. Whoops, I almost forgot, wasn't it Sr. Marie who taught us that it's not sucking, but the air pressure attempting to establish an equilibrium. Done, but it'll be a mess again as soon as the kids get home. I don't worry about that though because my adolescent psychology teacher said that was normal. So I've come to expect it.

1:00 p.m. My soap opera should be coming on just about now. I really enjoy it, as I can practice applying value judgments in different situations, just as in English. I can see what my reaction would be if I found out my daughter were pregnant, my husband divorced me, and my favorite store closed down, all in the same day.

Kids are home, and I'd better start making supper. Home economics comes in here. I know enough because of that class not to serve too many green foods in one meal. Mr. Lane's oriental philosophy class prepared me to keep an open mind when asked, "What's for supper?" During this busy time of the day my speech class comes in handy, "Bless us oh Lord and these thy gifts which we are about to receive through your bounty, through Christ our Lord. Amen."

It was hard for me to realize when I first took the courses, how much value they would have in my later life. But I was wrong. Every day I use them more and more. Why tomorrow I get to practice and discover new scientific methods of washing the dishes! I can't wait.

*Ann Cofell*
*St. Joseph, Minnetsota*

# THE INTERVIEW

The large metal clock read fifteen minutes until recess, and the consequent anxiety and restlessness of the pupils was evident in the room. During this period, the class had been divided into the usual three categories of reading groups, and as often is the case, the noise level of the class had become rather disruptive. Our teacher, between intermittent pleas for silence, was working with what we labeled the "low" reading group, seated in a circle with ten oral readers. Just as the class had become somewhat settled, the door opened and a man carrying a black briefcase entered our room. I do not remember the man's features at all, with the exception that, at first glance, he seemed rather tall and stocky.

After several minutes had passed, I heard my teacher calling my name and I looked up from my reading. She motioned for me to join them at the doorway and as I approached, she introduced us. "This is Mr. ——. (I never really listen to introductions.) He would like you to go with him for a little while, all right?"

From the moment of our introduction, I could feel my heart beat increasing and I remember a cold, penetrating chill circulating in my chest. I had no idea as to why the man wanted to see me, and as the introduction began, I recall considering all the possible reasons for this man's interest in me. My first reaction was that he had to be one of the speech therapists who occasionally interview students during class time. I immediately recalled, however, that I had never heard any mention of my having a speech problem, and as a matter of fact, being a member of the "high" reading group, felt assured that this was impossible. Searching for another answer, I felt convinced that I had unknowingly committed some horrendous offense, and was now being summoned to receive my punishment. My subsequent thoughts revolved around possible mistakes I could have made during the past week and a concise review of my behavior during the recent lunch periods. An amazing aspect of fear is the fleeting speed in which one can consider all aspects of a situation. After the several seconds of our introduction, I looked toward my teacher, who leaned against a wall adjoining the door. She was smiling warmly, as if nothing were at all abnormal about his presence, and then added, "I'll see you in a little while."

He then led me outside and we began walking down the corridor. By this time my entire body was shaking, and I was nervously fingering my sweater as we walked. I felt incredibly alone and frightened at the vagueness of his presence, and I could not understand how my teacher had allowed me to be taken from the class. As we walked, I was developing pains in my chest and was unable to speak as a result of the rising lump in my throat. I remember the man smiling at me profusely, as if that might ease my discomfort. I never smiled back, nor could I relax enough to talk with or question him. I recall having an immense urge to break away from him and run back to my classroom, and I debated about it throughout the walk. My ultimate decision was that if I were to run from him, he would then have another, this time *deliberate*, count of maliciousness against me, and I wasn't willing to take that risk.

He stopped at the school bookroom, a crowded

eight by ten storage room layered with books and folders. He opened the door for me and I hesitantly obeyed, still contemplating a sudden break for freedom. The room was dusty and smelled heavily of must and static air. He brought me a classroom chair from one corner of the room, and then sat down behind a large grey desk facing me. As I sat down, I searched my surroundings. The door was shut tightly against the dark walls and the air felt slightly damp. Several feet from my seat, hundreds of books, magazines, and records were stacked solidly upon desks and chairs. While carefully examining the room, a bell sounded from the wall outside and the outer hallway was filled with an outpour of voices and shuffling feet. As I heard the vibrations of the recess bell and the muffled shouts from the corridor, I started to cry; then hurriedly tried to suppress the tears. After several minutes, returning my gaze to the man, I noticed he was sorting out several papers and attaching a paper clip to the pile. He looked toward me and tapped his papers on the desk. "Hello, Gail." His voice was loud and intense, and it was obvious that he expected a reply.

I cleared my throat and stiffened in my chair. My eyes were fixed on his papers. "Hi."

"I'm going to give you several tests which shouldn't take too long. You can let me know when you're ready.

I then had another sudden impulse to run from the room and I can recall even beginning to rise from my seat. I couldn't envision myself actually running from him. After several seconds, I responded, "Sure, I don't care." I was trying desperately to keep my voice steady and shield the trembling of my hands.

"Now we're going to begin by pretending we have a compass in front of us. I'm going to name several different compass directions—n, s, e, w—at one time, and you tell me which direction we'll eventually be facing. For example, Gail, . . . starting from north—go east twice and then north once." I didn't quite understand the logic behind this test but I answered the twenty or twenty-five questions as well as I could. This test lasted about thirty minutes and when he had finished, he asked me how I knew directions so well. I ignored him and began playing with the buttons on my sweater as he again began shuffling his papers.

"Ah, now I'm going to read several sentences to you and I want you to read them back to me starting with the last word." I was beginning to relax in my seat and felt more comfortable with his questions. He read about fifteen sentences which became progressively longer and more complex. I remember doing well until the fifth sentence, then completely forgetting the originals and becoming frustrated. This test also lasted about thirty minutes, and was followed by several others. I do not recall each of the tests, although I imagine there were totally about four or five. After each of them, he wrote several sentences on the papers and finally put them aside. He began staring thoughtfully at me. "Tell me, Gail . . . ." His voice was becoming unnaturally personable. "What's your favorite subject in school?"

I thought for a moment. "Spelling."

"Spelling," he repeated. "Why do you enjoy it?"

"Because I spell so well. I like memorizing where the letters go. My favorite words are 'vocabulary' and 'bibliography' because they're so long. You want to see? I'm really good."

He laughed for a moment. It sounded like an extremely cold laugh. Do you enjoy any *real* subjects, like science or history?"

"I like them all. I guess my favorite is math, because I like solving problems and then organizing them in the squares on the paper. I like things very neat and organized."

He immediately picked up the papers and wrote something at the bottom of a sheet. I suppose I was beginning to feel more daring, and when he looked up again I asked him why he was asking me these questions. I cannot remember his reply if he gave me one. I don't believe he did.

After several minutes, he looked up from his papers and stared at me. I began to get nervous and felt extremely uneasy. He looked at his sheet again.

"Gail, it says here that you want to be a boy." His tone was very low and demanding. I shifted in my seat and stared at him.

"Oh, does it?" I tried to maintain a defiant expression but found myself lowering my eyes as he continued staring at me.

"Why do you want to be a boy, Gail? Don't you like being a girl?" I hadn't mentioned this before, but there is also something very uncomfortable about having people repeatedly call you by your first name when you are unable to remember any part of theirs.

I felt my heart vibrating and I stiffened in my chair. I don't believe that I had ever come in such direct contact on the subject with someone that I didn't know, and I felt now as if I had just been found guilty of a crime. I started to reply, god only knows what I was going to say, but then stopped. Firstly, I wasn't quite sure that I knew the answer myself. Secondly, I was being forced to talk *up* to him, as if actually admitting or at least justifying my guilt, while he was not honestly interested in me as a person, merely the circumstances of my case. It would be impossible for me to have replied on his level, either in defense or agreement, as I had originally begun, so I then attempted to get off the subject as quickly as possible.

"Well .... I don't *really* want to. I just .... well .... I like short hair and boys can have short hair. That's why."

I looked around the silent room and stared at a row of books on the far shelf. The dust seemed to be standing motionless in the air, and I could not feel myself breathing. A table creaked in the far corner of the room. I looked back at the man's hard stare.

"Well, that's very simple, Gail. Why don't you just get a haircut?"

I stared at him. "Sure. That's it, yea. I'll just get a haircut. Yea, I'd really like one. O.K."

I assumed that my decision had succeeded in appeasing him, as he suddenly smiled broadly at me and said that there was really nothing to it.

The rest of the interview, as far as I remember, consisted of more questions about hobbies, television shows, and interests. There were many instances of his deadly stares and my smiling uneasily to avoid his gaze. After a total of two or two and a half hours, he allowed me to leave and walk back to class unescorted. I remember being terribly polite and gracious when I left. I think I even thanked him for everything. When I returned to class I didn't talk to anyone, and when I got home from school, I remember crying the entire day.

*Gail Eisen*
*Los Angeles, California*

# Roles

## PART II

*Lydia Sims*
*New York, New York*

# i am

i am a figment of my own imagination,
a reflection of my shadow,
i am what i eat.

i am a poem by emily dickinson,
a mad hatter, lost in wonderland,
each book i feast my eyes upon becomes a part of me.

i am a tree as it waltzes in the wind,
or an apple, clinging cautiously to its branch,
teasing, tempting me to take a bite.

i am a glamorous star, swooning on the screen,
an ancient woman huddled in a doorway,
a tiny infant as it savors the sweetness of its
mother's breast.

i am a wart nestled between your fingers,
a freckle which kisses your forehead,
the apple of your eye.

*Jessica Teich*
*Huntington, New York*

# ELEGY TO MYSELF

Never ask who i am
i am page 7 of the newspaper
or the part between commercials
at 6 o'clock, 10 o'clock, 11 o'clock
i am the mother who doesn't know
where her children are
i am Belfast blood, Boston blood, Brooklyn blood
i am a cop, a college girl, a storekeeper
or an Olympic athlete
i am an elderly woman afraid to leave my house
a bird in a gilded cage
i am a passer-by, i, too, am a victim
robbed, mugged, harassed, knifed, raped, beaten
kidnapped, dead instantly, dead on arrival
or much later
never ask who i am
the paragraphs in the paper are always there
inevitably
the names are always your name.

*Dina Grussgott*
*Brooklyn, New York*

# WHEN I READ POETRY

sometimes
when i read
poetry—i get
hurt
because somebody stole
my idea—
but i think
it's mostly that
i realize
that
sometimes
i have to hear
other people's
words
to realize
what
i feel.

*Lauri London*
*North Hollywood, California*

# ONLY OF WORDS

My own plastic laughter rings in my ears
as escaping,
        I travel many miles
Seeking into my depths.
        You know me well?
Ha! These sentences aren't mine,
For my walls, stronger than those of
        cement
are made only of words.
        Hiding behind them,
My tears are masked as smiles.

*Roberta Rebold*
*Roslyn Heights, New York*

# "WHEN, AT THE RIPE OLD AGE OF 16 . . ."

*When, at the ripe old age of 16, I decided that I was just plain sick and tired of being a teenager, I knew that I would have to change my image.* Alas, it is much easier to *say* that you will change your image than it is to actually do so, especially if you have no choice of occupation or social status. My alternatives were clear-cut. I could become a young adult, which would entail the taking on of more responsibility and the wearing of sensible shoes; I could become a juvenile delinquent, which would mean becoming impertinent to my elders; skipping classes and shoplifting; I could become a hippie, in which case I would have to forgo baths, start an organic garden and limit my vocabulary to, "Peace and love, brothers and sisters!"; I could become a pothead, which I couldn't afford; or I could become an adolescent—a teenager with problems.

Naturally, it was the latter classification which appealed to me, since the only changes I would have to make would be mental. I set about the task of readying myself for the "big day." My preparation completed, I knew that I could do it.

The "big day" dawned clear and beautiful. I lay in bed until my mother came in.

"It's a beautiful day. Time to get up."

"Smelvertikizatomskrin," I muttered.

"What?"

"I said, 'In your estimation it is a beautiful day.' But I know that the torment inside one's head can turn any day into a living nightmare that could produce traumatic side effects on the young mind."

"Get up now or you'll miss your bus."

At breakfast I realized that I would have to strengthen my character. So I said to the plastic daisies in the center of the table: " 'A rose by any other name would smell as sweet.' But you, you fools—you were born as plastic flowers whose destinies are not even that of the ugly duckling. You must suffer in your styrofoam-filled flowerpots with dust caked in layers on your molded plastic personalities. You may argue that Fate made you what you are, but I say—Be strong! Fight Fate! You can be what you want to be; do what you want to do! Do not sit there and calmly accept your given place in life. Fight for your ideals! Fight!!!"

"Quiet, dear, you'll wake your sister."

"Have you no compassion in your heart for the fate of—"

"Here's your lunch money. Let the cat in on your way out." Mothers are hard-hearted creatures at seven in the morning.

After first period was over at school, I made my way to my locker and put on my mittens. Then I went to the library to do my homework. Some friends came by as I struggled, pen in mitten.

"You oughta use gloves if your hands are cold," I was told.

"That would defeat the purpose," I said sourly.

"If the purpose is to get an F in penmanship, so it would," said someone.

"No, no, no. You see, I am psychologically handicapped. My cold fingers are a manifestation of a life without love, without communication, without understanding. I must take my life in my own hands. But I cannot give up hope, not yet. I must reach out to society, send out some signal to those people who might still have some compassion left in their souls.

"Through this writing they will see my impediment. They will look past the meaningless facade of my answer, 'I'm all right,' and go straight to my unspoken plea for help."

"You're gonna get an F in penmanship."

It must be working, I thought to myself. After all, nobody understands an adolescent. As I walked down the hall on my way to lunch, I felt my eyes filling with tears. Very good, I congratulated myself. You're becoming an expert adolescent.

A few people noticed my puffy red eyes, but they didn't say anything. (To me, anyway.) Finally, just as the tears fell, a guidance counselor happened down my hall.

"There, there, what is it?" she asked compassionately, putting a patronizing arm around my shoulder.

I jerked violently away, gritting my teeth and saying, "You wouldn't understand. It's—it's—just nothing." I waited for her to retaliate.

"Now, now. People don't cry for 'just nothing.' You can tell me. I was your age once myself."

"Things are different now. There's more pressure on us today. And now, when you find out that—that—" I sobbed a little louder.

"Come, come, there's no need for those tears. It couldn't be that bad. You just need to talk it over."

"I can't! Why don't you understand that I just *can't*! I can't let anyone else know just how awful it is, because soon everyone would know, and if everyone knew, life just wouldn't be worth living. I just can't let them know. I can't break their pitifully naive, yet very happy bubbles of ignorance. I MUST BEAR THE BURDEN ALONE!"

"Well . . . !" I was about to congratulate her on saying "Well" instead of "Well, well," but I didn't want to break the suspense. So I ran down the hall, sobbing to myself, carrying my burden and my mittens to the girls' room.

After a while, my eyes were once again their pale color. So I headed towards the cafeteria where some of my adolescent friends were waiting.

"I heard you had a run-in with a guidance person," I was greeted.

"Yeah. They do it out of a sense of obligation to mankind," I said.

"You O.K. now?"

"Life is but a bowl of avocadoes, my friends," said yours truly with a twinkle in her eye. "One must always remember that we were placed on this earth for the sole purpose of learning how to fill out an income tax form. It is only when we have legally obtained our tax refunds that we will find our lives fulfilled."

"That's too heavy for me," said one.

"What significance is there to such a life?" queried another.

"How could one lead such an empty, meaningless existence?" inquired yet a third.

"Yours is not to question why; yours is but to do or die," I said by way of enlightenment.

"That's just too heavy, man. Gotta give some deep thought to that."

With that I left them. My first day as a bonafide adolescent was drawing to a close. Back at home after a hard day at school, I announced to my family that I wasn't going to do my homework because it was "irrelevant to my lifestyle." I was then given the task of convincing my little brother that homework WAS relevant to HIS lifestyle.

Five P.M. found me trying to play my guitar left-handed and studying Bangladesh's problems in the *National Geographic*, muttering all the while about how unfair it (whatever "it" refers to) is. I skipped dinner, with the explanation to my family that my body is of the young, hardy variety, and that it becomes necessary to enforce self-discipline.

As my bedtime rolled around, I realized that nobody understood me. I vowed to become even less comprehensible on the 'morrow, and fell fast asleep.

Dawn of the second day of my new role as an adolescent brought with it clouds and drizzles. I lay in bed wondering about just what it is that income tax involves when my mother came in to wake me up.

"It's a miserable day, time to get up," she said, poking me in the side.

I got up feeling unbelievably cheerful. (I always do when it rains.) I said nothing as I sat down to breakfast. Then I saw a plastic daisy wink at me.

"You win," I said, digging into my raisin bran.

"What?" said my Mom.

"Bleinsletvorskoratizomkrick."

"It's good to have you back, dear."

*Karen McRobie*
*Thornwood, New York*

# THE CROW

It came down quietly, and Diana was so absorbed in thought that she never noticed it until it perched on her arm.

"Oh!" she exclaimed in surprise. "Why, you're a crow, aren't you? So beautiful, too!"

Indeed, it was beautiful. Jet-black, with a grey beak and green eyes like a cat. It was smooth and soft; in every possible way, it resembled the creatures that Diana so loved.

"Where are you from?" Diana found herself wishing the bird could answer.

The crow, for it was a crow, gently lifted itself into the sky, as if to answer her. Diana watched in awe, her eyes fixed on the graceful movement of his wings. She watched as he circled smoothly and landed silently near her hand.

"Joshua," she said. "May I call you Joshua?" She looked into the bird's eyes and felt a yearning inside her. She wanted to call him her own, to teach him her secrets and to be his friend.

"Joshua, come closer. Come here. Joshua, would you like to stay with me? Joshua, I want you."

She spoke softly, her voice gently lulling the bird. And he understood. He came nearer and nearer, until he was within the reach of her slim hands.

She reached slowly towards the bird and wrapped her hands around it. It tried to escape once, but she only held tighter. Rising, she carried it to the garage and opened the door of a cage. Carefully she placed the crow into it, and shut the door.

"The cat won't care if I use her travel-box. She hates it, anyway." Then she ran into the house to tell her mother.

"Oh, Diana. You've got to let it go. You know what happened to the others!"

"But, Mom, Joshua . . . he's different! He wants to!" Diana walked out of the kitchen, but her mother followed, pleading.

"Diana, you can't keep it. He'll die, like Jeremy and Veronica and Caesar did. He can't live in captivity!"

"Mom, he's so . . . so graceful, so free! I found him and he's mine!" She ran up to her room and locked the door.

The next day Diana took her new pet for a walk—in the cage. She saw him glance longingly at the sky, but ignored it. "He'll get over it soon," she thought. Weeks went by, though, and Joshua still longed for the open sky. Diana ignored his struggling attempts to gain his freedom.

"Joshua, you don't want to go, do you?" she would say. "You like it here, don't you? You'll always be here. You love it. I know you do."

"She gets worse every day, doctor. I don't know what to do! She sits in her room, or with that bird . . . Joshua, she calls it . . . . Yes, three other birds, but . . . . It's like a wall separates her from humanity . . . . No, she doesn't even speak to me . . . . Doctor, what can I do?"

"Well, Mrs. Simms, the problem may be the bird. She may be . . . in love with it, in a sense . . . Serious? Not really. The solution is simple enough . . . Let the bird go."

"No!" Diana was hysterical when her mother told her what the doctor had said. She ran out of the house, screaming, and into the garage.

"No, never! He's my Joshua! He loves me! No, never!"

She opened the cage and grabbed Joshua. She flew as far as her legs would carry her, away from the house. Then she sat down, sobbing.

"Joshua. Oh, Joshua! They . . . they want to . . ." Her voice was cut off by sobs. "Joshua, you want to stay, don't you? Do you want to stay here, or leave? Please, Joshua, say you'll stay!"

Joshua struggled violently to get free from Diana's grasp. He cawed, and another bird answered.

Looking into the sky, Diana saw a bird through misty eyes. It curved gracefully and landed near them. A female, she thought. She wants my Joshua. She wants to steal my Joshua. But then a voice inside her finally came to the surface. It had been there ever since she first saw Joshua flying free in the sky. It cried out; it pleaded; it screamed.

Let him go! If he really loves you, he will stay. He is free, and he deserves a chance to leave if he wants to. If you love him, give him a chance at the freedom he was born with, the freedom you took from him and that he deserves. Let him go! The voice grew. She heard it, and she listened silently. It pleaded with her. She was torn between her love for Joshua and that voice. He loved her, didn't he? Or did he? Slowly, slowly she loosened her hold and removed her hands from his soft body. He turned to her, as if to say "Thank you," and then he spread his wings and flew.

It was as if spring had suddenly appeared, giving everything a new chance at life. The crow soared silently, gliding on the wind. He circled expertly and called. His mate rose into the air and joined him. Together they flew off into the distance, as the wind blew in the pines.

Just as they passed from view, the crow called,

and Diana understood. He was grateful. She had done the right thing. Her heart had left with Joshua, but she had been right. He deserved to be free, as did the others. He deserved to have a mate of his own kind.

He was free, and he had been robbed of his freedom. She was free, but she had infringed on his freedom. Freedom was a delicate thing, she thought, and if it were abused, it became a monster. She had abused her freedom, she saw, but now everything was right again.

Diana rose silently as tears formed in her eyes. She went home and ran to her room without even a nod to the cat. Taking a pencil and paper, she scrawled some words and, dropping onto her bed, cried. The words on her pad were the following:

THE CROW

He came silently and perched
On my arm, and I thought
That he said to me:
Be my master, my love.
But I was wrong, for
His soul wished to be free.

But I took him,
And loved him.
And I left the human race,
And became like a crow.

But it was not enough.

He flew away silently.
And silently I wished him love
And returned
To my real world,
Longing to be free like the crow.

*Debra Ziehm*
*Phoenix, Arizona*

## WOMEN

Women
about women
for women
of women
is, after all,
just people.

*Laura Gordon*
*Rolling Hills Estates,*
*California*

## MIRRORS

I look in my mirror
everyday
I try to fit my image
whatever that may be.
Dreams take me over
and I lose contact with the mirror
I am now seeing myself
staring at my own reflection.
Funny how I've always pictured myself
as a walking oddity
something for one to stare at
when waiting for a bus
or doing something of less importance.
Trying on different expressions.
Practicing for people
hoping no one will see.

*Reiko Obata*
*San Diego, California*

# CASTLES

Some build castles of precious gems
that glisten and burn in the summer sun.
Others build castles of stone to protect
themselves against the winds of the wilderness.
But I build castles of sand that sift into the sea
and become alienated to me.

*Cheryll Galvin*
*Omaha, Nebraska*

# ANALYSIS

freud
says
falling
dreams
are common
to rural
and urban
children alike

i don't fall
from extreme
heights
in my dreams
as he says
i should

i

jump

*Randy Mott*
*Skaneateles, New York*

# BLESSING

It is not a blessing
to be able to turn
and look inward
at yourself.
You reflect
as others reflect,
And you see
as others see.
You know the wrongs
of which others
accuse you
before they are
brought to mind,
And you live
knowing them,
feeling them,
keeping them
hidden, you hope.
But others see deeply
also,
so they must be
hidden deeply,
Or erased.
People see scars
and marks
even
where we fail to look.
It is not a blessing
to be able to turn
And say
This is me.

*Cathy Ferrand*
*Interlaken, New York*

# lorda

lorda became a waitress out of fear. she put on her uniform over her obsessions with dark eyes and rum, the man who made music, and the man who made love and no sense. she put her tips in her pocket with the songs she made for the man who drove his sports car out of her life at the end of the week. she sang the songs from her gut until the smile from the corner booth had emptied her out. after closing time, she made music of words for the man who made magic with music. the words refused to fill her efficient cold eyes. lorda became bitter after hours, waiting for the man who drove an old truck. she emptied her pockets of tips and obsessions with white shoes. the man who took her to drink beer and see movies became angry, having finally discovered her gut, to find her empty. he left the state muttering revisions of obsessions with harmony, and lorda became a person, out of work.

in summer, lorda became a carpenter out of school. she put nails in sheetrock and in her mouth and drove nails along obsessions with spackle and straight lines. she became a perfectionist out of habit. lorda made measurements for the man who made the cuts and she laughed past her dusty hair in the day. a room began to materialize out of nails and sheetrock and spackle, dust and beer in the afternoon. lorda began to materialize out of ancient lath.

lorda washed dust out of her hair in the evening. she became happy among lumber. she made songs, after evenings, for the man who was sad and sang the songs with a smile until the man who was lonely took her life in the street. she picked most of it up, and dusted most of it off. she gave a little of what was left to the man who was worried about her, and sewed the rest into the lining of her jacket when she walked. she walked always with friends and with obsessions, with lonely men and dark hillsides.

lorda became angry out of necessity. she drank tea and anger and obsessions with music and muscles and hate. she made songs for herself and sang them for herself and for the man who cared. she made music with the lady who wore ruffles and fur, until the lady became a fortune seeker out of state. lorda made music alone out of old obsessions with harmony. the man who cared became old harmony and lorda made new harmony with the lady who drank tequilla out of the bottle. they made music with friends, for hundreds of people, for several people, for themselves, until the lady followed the man who made the music. alone again, lorda stayed just far enough away from the man who made magic out of clay. alone, lorda got close to obsessions with closeness. near to it, she put laughing and well-vagued words in the way, among wine. lorda became distant out of habit. once trapped among obsessions with distance, lorda woke up screaming out of dreams.

*Kathie Merrill*
*Plainfield, Vermont*

# THE INNOCENCE OF MY GUILT

"She's dead. She was my closest friend and now she's dead, and I killed her.

"She'll never be the actress or renowned criminal lawyer or the winner of the Nobel Prize.

"—Was that a siren!" No! it couldn't be, I've listened hard and nobody heard or nobody cared. There will be no body, no trace of what happened here today.

"She's gone forever but I'm not to blame; it was bound to happen, you know. Did she really think she could get away with that.

"Her with her high honor, high horse attitude, her sweet virginal smile which cowed all the teachers. It's enough to make you sick. She *is*, no she *was* so shy and disgustingly cute.

"Did she really think I'd let her oppose me without a fight.

"The showdown had to be. She couldn't say those things; she couldn't call me a fool and a stupid idiot and a common whore and get away with it, no way.

"But I'm not confessing; I didn't kill her. She killed herself; she was at fault. She must have wanted to die being the way she was.

"She did it all to herself and now she has even less than she started with, if she started with anything at all.

"I must get rid of her corpse and get her out of my mind. I must rid myself of her memory forever.

"I just can't stand looking in the mirror and seeing me, her killer, standing beside her victim, . . . ME."

*Donna Churchill*
*Rocky Hill, Connecticut*

# "TINKY"

He looked at me, never winking once. He acted as if he knew that I couldn't outstare him, and I couldn't. I gave up trying. Nevertheless, I liked to look in his eyes for as long as I could. His eyes were like two topaz stones, brighter than the sun (at least to me), with two coal black dots in the middle. I loved that cat, and I felt my heart breaking in two. My mother always thought it best to put old animals out of their miseries. It was time for Tinky and me to separate, never to meet again, or so I thought.

From what I could see, Tinky was much like myself. We both had that dull, disconcerting expression. Once in a while, I could have sworn that I saw Tinky smile, as if he were thinking to himself, as I often did. All in all, he was a selfish cat, but I loved him for it, maybe because I was a selfish person.

I argued with my parents on several occasions about this matter, but it never seemed to do any good. An old animal should be put to sleep, and that was that, they said. They were just about as stubborn as I was. I even tried making several threats; for instance, running away; hiding away so that they couldn't find me; hunger strikes; etc. Well by now, you should have an idea about how much I loved that cat.

When the vet came, I ran into the bathroom. I was so used to running in there when I couldn't get my way. I locked the door, and decided to stay there until she left. After a while, I heard the metal cage open, and after a moment's hesitation, close again. It was then that I decided to come out. Before the cage locked, I rushed to it, picked up Tinky, kissed him on the snowy white valentine shape of his head, and set him down inside the cage again. I handled his sleek black body (except for the valentine), with tender care, as if he were a piece of fragile glass, in a glass menagerie. The vet bent down and locked the cage while I ran back into the bathroom before she could say anything.

I sat in the bathroom, and thought of various ways to avenge the cat, and get even with my parents. They don't put any old people out of their misery. Anyway, I don't see that Tinky was in so much misery. I was the one in misery. It was true that all he did now was eat, and sleep. He didn't even chase mice any more. I've had him ever since I was a year old. He was old for 16, and I was still young for 16. Since I was an only child, he was my only companion. I didn't have too many friends.

I finally decided to stop acting like a child, and come out of the bathroom. I also decided to stop speaking to either one of my parents, for at least two weeks. I headed straight for the front door. "What's the matter; cat got your tongue?" asked my father. I glanced at him with sharp cold eyes. I was waiting for my mother to ask me where I was going. I got to feeling worse, because SHE DIDN'T EVEN BOTHER TO ASK. As I slammed the door, I heard the windows rattle from inside. There was no one around, and nothing to do, so I finally gave up and went back into my house.

I awoke early the next morning. The sun's rays played a game of hide and seek on the back of my scorched neck. I decided to start this beautiful summer morning off right, even though I was a little angry. I began by taking a cold shower, which I usually don't do, at least not a cold one. I then got dressed, in dungarees, as usual. I ate whatever I could find in the refrigerator, cleaned up my dusty room, and headed for the door. As I was going out, my parents were going into the kitchen. "Just where do you think you're going this early?"

I didn't answer my mother; I just shrugged my shoulders. I could tell she was a little annoyed at me at this point, so I tried not to be so sassy. She continued, "I've had enough of your childish actions, and I'm going to put a stop to this, now!"

She grabbed at me, but I bolted out of the door before she could get a good grip on me. She didn't come after me, and I was a great deal relieved. I could hear her and my father laughing inside. I was spoiled, and I knew it. They knew it also. They always gave me what I wanted, except for this time.

I just hung around outside until about eleven o'clock. Just before I entered the building, I noted a faint odor of what seemed like chloroform. I paid no attention to it. The hallways of the building were deserted. I pressed for the elevator for about thirty minutes. I then got disgusted, and started for the stairs. When I opened the exit door, the smell of chloroform became overpowering. I felt my knees weakening. I thought I was going to collapse. I ran out of the exit coughing, almost choking. I went to the other exit. I covered my nose and my mouth with my hands, and decided to make a run for it. I felt a presence behind me, which made me stop dead in my tracks.

Standing there, with his back arched, and his hair standing on end, was Tinky. I was so overjoyed, I ran to him, completely forgetting about the odor of the chloroform, which seemed to get stronger as I approached him. My hand went through the misty figure, and hit the cold graffiti-covered wall. I started up the stairs again. When I looked this time, he was at the top of the stairs, spitting and fuming at me. The way the cat acted, I was afraid to pass him. I ran out of the exit again, and took the elevator, which was already there. I didn't stop to answer my parents' questions; I went straight to my room and talked myself to sleep.

The next morning, I heard the news. The girl across the hall, whom I knew but slightly, and whose mother was my mother's best friend, was killed on the third floor, at about eleven-fifteen. She, too, had not intended to walk up the stairs. My mother was tearfully telling the vet, who had come to bring back Tinky's collar, all of this.

"People can't walk the streets at night anymore."

"Yeah, I know what you mean," the vet nodded in agreement. She then handed the collar to me, and added, "You know that cat acted so calm, until about eleven, or around that time. Then he began to spit and jump at the wall for what seemed like no reason. You know, they say animals can smell, and see death. Do you believe that's true Mrs. Carlton?" My mother was much too busy watching the expression on my face. The vet then noticed it too. I explained what had happened to me the previous night. They both listened, in quiet consternation.

Then they started talking again. I drowned out the sound of their talking with my thoughts. The murdered girl could have been I. That's why Tinky didn't want me to go up the stairs; he knew what was waiting for me; he was protecting me, even when he was near death. In my mind, I thanked Tinky (even though I was sorry for the other girl), and silently, but surely, thanked God.

*Roslyn James*
*New York, New York*

# IS MY MIND

*I*

The still and stagnant morning;
the dew-wet morning
without sun
is my mind.
Solitary expanse of morning
is my mind.
Big sky country,
blue-gray morning
centuries old:
    lying on stone ground—
    cold ground—
    earth—
    a silver thought—
    weaves through my mind.
Sadness is realization,
not manifestation;
    rolling over
leave me be
that I may break the stone.

*II*

This is not a lament,
I am not this country.
My mind is motionless
fixed upon the cosmos.
What I am
is not my mind.
What—
what share of me
is my mind?

What part:
  experience
  emotion
  intellect
  development
  link—
    a process
    a means to an end
    that governs not,
and no more.

*Laura Gordon*
*Rolling Hills Estates,*
*California*

# AT TIMES

Sooner or later,I am told,I will be wiser.

Rumplestiltskin hammered himself into the ground,
or like a
screw,gyrated six feet deep.He's there now,a blemish of
his breed,a hang-nail of earth.At times,I wonder too if my
descent will be so sure,certain and with such a rhythm:
Bur-ied a-live,bur-ied a-live—young and sweet and
bur-ied a-live.

I'm no goldenlocked female,hanging tepid from
parapets.When
leaning from my window,I whistle to the street at times
and the whistles return.Blush,retreat.No porridge tales of
marriage.Just blush,retreat,feel foolish.

At times,the question of whose hammer comes to bend
around
my mind and down into such a mind that wonders at times.

At times,I'm like this:
When crossing a large field,someone is at one side,waving
good bye.One leg wants to go back and jerks a bit,the other
forward.And like that line people quote about,at times I
think the waves are cries for help.

History,at times sadly enough,speaks for itself and the
waving becomes a cry for hope,as I move on.

*Jennifer Crichton*
*New York, New York*

# HERE'S TO YOU, MOTHER

"Here's to you, mother," I said
and I raised my glass high
and then slammed it
onto the table.
Slowly,
the glass shattered
and the beer she told me ladies never drink
spat in her eye.
"I am tired," I told her,
"I am tired of being a small
grotesque china doll that you dress
in spiderweb lace and satin peignoir.

I am tired of being told
what ladies do
and what they don't and
I am tired of being told
that lady is not synonymous with woman.

Please,
I'm not a china doll,
I'm real, real, real . . .

*Sue Doherty*
*Mineola, New York*

# LISA'S PRAYER

one day, i shall fit my own definition:
i will laugh freely and talk loudly;
i will play as hard as i can;
& sometimes i'll play harder than the boys.
i'll do anything i want, if i think it's okay,
i will be Free:
the chains . . . shoulds and shouldn'ts
will break
yes . . . by God! . . . I'll be Lisa . . . me . . . no one else
and i'll know I'm okay
some day . . .
Please.

*Lisa Berman*
*Merrick, New York*

# THE WESTERN KID GOES EAST

I'm a Western kid, but mostly just because I was born there and lived there for what seemed like an awful long time. I'm not so Western anymore, but sometimes I wish I were, so I could run around telling people that when I die, I want to be buried up on Rebel Hill above Canyon City, Oregon, population six hundred and thirty, where gold was discovered in 1862. There was some excitement around there then, I guess. Rebel Hill got named one night when a bunch of miners got drunk at Sel's Brewery, and one bunch of them took over Rebel Hill while the other bunch tried to get it away from them. It's hard to say what they were fighting about, but they were all drunk and pounding on each other with big sticks and broken bottles, and I guess nobody ever did figure out who won. It's mostly quiet there now, except for Debbie Thomason's little brother Jerry who set our pear tree on fire once.

I don't especially want to be buried up on Rebel Hill anymore, and sometimes it makes me feel like a traitor to my homeland. I don't really care where I get buried as long as I'm not in anybody's way. I don't even care if they dig me up to put in a super highway, as long as they don't put it up on Rebel Hill. I do have that much loyalty. But if they did decide to build a super highway up on Rebel Hill, I guess I'd just say, "Well, maybe Debbie Thomason's little brother Jerry will get hit by a truck, and they can bury him up Bear Creek until they put in a super highway up there." I used to think a lot about getting buried up on Rebel Hill. I also used to think a lot about Debbie Thomason's little brother Jerry getting hit by a truck, but I guess that doesn't necessarily have anything to do with being a Westerner.

It seems like ever since I was born I've been thinking about getting buried up on Rebel Hill, and I always thought that when I was born was a long time ago, but according to the authorities on the matter it hasn't been so long. Maybe it just seems like a long time ago because I don't like to think about where I was born. The only thing I remember about the place is how I learned to hate buttermilk. I've learned to like it since, of course, but it hardly ever cheers me up to look in the mirror and say to myself, "Now there's a real Westerner, born an awful long time ago in Gilroy, California, the garlic capital of the world." So much for good beginnings.

Once a year in Canyon City, Oregon, they open up Sel's Brewery to celebrate the gold discovery of 1862, and everyone gets rippin' drunk. They always tar and feather someone and hang someone. Once they even ran someone out of town on a rail. They're always having shoot-outs in Sel's Brewery, and it's lots of fun. There's always a beard contest, and any man without a beard gets thrown in the Greenhorn Jail and gets his picture taken. Once they threw a Senator in there, and I was surprised he didn't declare Canyon City, Oregon, a disaster area right on the spot.

During the festivities, Canyon City is called Whiskey Gulch because that's what it was called back in the good old days when Rebel Hill was getting its name and they were throwing guys in the Greenhorn Jail for real if they overdid things a little at Sel's Brewery. It must have been fun hanging around Whiskey Gulch watching all those miners stagger out of Sel's Brewery on their way up to

Rebel Hill to pound on each other with big sticks and broken bottles. Tourists still go up there sometimes with metal detectors and find old belt buckles. I don't know exactly what those guys were doing up on Rebel Hill that made them leave so many belt buckles lying around, but I guess that doesn't have much to do with being a Westerner, either.

I don't feel much like a Westerner anymore, except that I know about rattlesnakes and coyotes. People in the East seem to think that coyotes are like wolves, but they're not really. They don't even sound like wolves. I know because I used to listen to them howling on the other side of the valley before I went to sleep, and on the ranch they'd come pretty close to the house sometimes after dark. Coyotes don't have near as much going for them as wolves do. They're not very big to start with, but if you shoot one that's trying to chew on one of your cows or your clothesline or something (coyotes will eat anything), and you skin him, you'll end up with whole bunches of coyote hair, about ten pounds of rattly red wire meat and some bones. I know because I had to skin a coyote once and take the meat off the bones for a science project in the eighth grade and I got an A.

Coyotes don't have much going for them at all. The Air Force wants to get about twelve thousand coyotes and use all those whole bunches of coyote hair to line flight jackets with. It's a hard life in the West. Even for rattlesnakes. Jim, the big Indian hired man on the ranch, used to kill rattlesnakes exclusively with a twenty-two rifle, and I never saw him miss except once. That didn't really count since it was because I gave him a dud bullet. Jim could also run out into a field and grab a calf and get back to the haywagon with it before the mother cow got to him. That's tricky business, too. I know because a mother cow came after me once and there's a fence on the ranch that I still hold the all-time record for getting over in the shortest time. I wasn't quite so lucky with the mother hen, but that's only because there was no fence.

I guess rattlesnakes are the only really truly Westerners, except maybe for Mary who used to do our ironing sometimes. She had a crusty little husband named Jack who taught me how to roll cigarettes and got mad when I put tape on them because there wasn't any glue on the papers. Mary had a funny little dog, too, who was a lot like Jack, and she used to call me Miss all the time. Mary really has lived in the West for a long time. I know because she used to tell me stories about ironing in the Chinese laundry for ten cents an hour and eloping with Jack in a horse and buggy. She told me where the old highway was and where there's another old highway since then, and that there's no more Chinese laundry because the Chinese left when the gold miners left. They used to work hard for the gold miners for not very much money. Mary must be a really truly Westerner because she's the only person I know who's never even considered being anything else. I interviewed her once for a history project in the eighth grade. She told me about the Chinese graveyard and I got an A. They didn't put a super highway on the Chinese graveyard. They put a hospital and a trailer park on it instead. The Chinese didn't have much going for them. At least the Air Force didn't decide to make them into flight jackets.

Mary took me horseback riding on her brother's ranch after I recovered from my first attack of mezenteric lymph adenitis. That's a fancy name for messed up glands, I guess, but it just felt like a twelve pound sledge hammer to me. I woke up doubled over at four in the morning. Mary was taking care of us for the weekend because Mom and Dad had gone off to the coast to celebrate their anniversary. I didn't want to wake her up so I crawled into the bathroom to take some aspirin and went back to bed. In the morning I still couldn't stand up, but Mary didn't get upset at all. She just said I should take some more aspirin as it was probably something I ate. By afternoon I could stand up almost straight again and off we went in Jack's old green pickup, just as Mary had promised. We had a grand old time, and I really appreciated the way Mary handled the situation a lot more than what happened after my second attack of mezenteric lymph adenitis. It happened a week after the first one and I woke up doubled over at four in the morning.

My father, the doctor, is a handy sort of fellow to have around, except that it was pretty hard to get away with a fake stomach ache when I didn't want to go to school. Anyway, he took me to the hospital for some X-rays. It would have been all right, too, except that, before I knew it, they had me in one of those little dinky nightgowns and every doctor in the place was coming in to poke my stomach. I should have gotten suspicious, because they kept saying "aha" all the time and rubbing their chins, but, I never did, until a nurse came in and started shaving off all of the hair below my navel. I got a little upset because there wasn't much there anyway, and when I asked her how come she was doing that, she just smiled her little nurse smile and wouldn't say a thing. Anyway, the X-rays turned out to be surgery, and that would have been all right except that the surgery turned into two weeks laid off from swim team practice, right at the height of the season. The next year I got the measles. It's a hard life in the West.

I guess Mary got pretty upset when she found out she'd taken me horseback riding when what I needed all along was surgery. But being in the hospital was all right because a lot of people came to see me and brought presents and flowers and cards. Dan, the poet, brought me a card made of an A & W napkin that said, "Watch out for your doctor . . . he has inside information." I think it had a picture of some stitches, and I thought it was disgusting. None of the nurses would put any ice in my water because they said it would put air in my stomach. When my father came around, I told him about it and he said it was just an old wives' tale. I don't know how wives keep getting blamed for all the old tales that turn out to be a bunch of baloney, but my father got me some ice, anyway, which was what I was mainly concerned with at the time.

They gave me tea and jello, mostly, when my stomach finally stopped objecting every time I tried to put something in it, but they gave me a lot of injections, too, and I went home looking like a pincushion. The jello was always warm and the tea always tasted soggy. I've noticed that Westerners don't drink much tea except when they're in the hospital. I drank six cups of tea a day for a whole year after I moved East, but that wasn't until after I decided I didn't want to get buried up on Rebel Hill.

*Kathie Merrill*
*Plainfield, Vermont*

# THE PIANIST

As she struck the opening chord of the Brahms Rhapsody, her mind flashed back to the summer when she had first studied the piece. Her fingers went their own way, climbing and stumbling over the black keys towards the crescendo; but her mind followed another melody.

She hummed to herself, folded the underwear and placed it back on the shelf. She estimated how long it had been since her break, then glanced at the clock. The time crept by, and at the end of the day it seemed as if she'd done nothing for eight hours. It was the repetition. Nothing could seem quite as endless as piling and repiling shirts the month-end sale crowd had pawed over. She could not account for the time; every minute was like the next.

"You're working too hard. Let me see your hand." The department store guard lifted her hand from her side, shook his head and walked away.

Her eyes stole toward the clock again, and she grinned to herself. Five more minutes over and done with. She had to work five hours stocking boxer shorts and briefs to pay for a half hour lesson. Another five hours of stocking polo shirts and "t-shirts for the tall man" would give her sixty minutes with her teacher.

"Let me see your hand again." The department store guard was back. "Don't put those pins in your mouth, or I'll be afraid to kiss you when we get married." He laughed and walked away.

She didn't mind the work when she felt she was being useful. But everything was so disorganized. And it wasn't just the customers' fault.

They came in and opened packages and mixed the sizes; but the clerks didn't know where anything was either. She knew well the pressure of time and this store was inefficiently run and organized. Everyone thought her slightly fanatical, but she knew precision and efficiency were worthwhile in the end.

The guard was back. He wordlessly lifted her hand, looked at it; then patted it reassuringly.

"Just making sure the wedding ring I'm going to buy you fits."

She made a face at his back as he walked away. He epitomized all the blocks in her way. His job as a guard was the same day after day—no growing or changing involved, no new ideas to explore. And those dumb flirting games he played with her! Of course, it flattered her, but it also disgusted her. What satisfaction could one get from being someone's object? Had he ever met an obstacle and overcome it to achieve that great feeling of near perfection? Had he ever pushed and driven himself hard to reach a goal? He exemplified the store and all it was, and at that moment she hated it.

He ambled over again, and slowly pushed a pair of underwear into place in an attempt to look useful.

"You want to see a movie after work tonight?"

"No . . . . I have to practice the piano."

"Well, how about tomorrow?"

"I can't . . . ever. I practice every night."

"Oh, I see," he said disbelievingly, thinking she was playing games with him. "Who do you think you are anyway," he mumbled.

Her hands seemed stiff on the last chords and she slurred the few ending notes, her mind being elsewhere. Now she turned back to the present and what was before her. She got up from the bench and looked out towards the rows and rows of empty seats in the large hall. Tomorrow was the opening night of her concert series and it was already sold out. Her determination and concentration were in top form. She would play marvelously and the "remarkable young pianist whose hands sparkled over the keys like the master Rubenstein" would triumph in her own right.

*Sylvia Quintessence Sensiper*
*Los Angeles, California*

# THOUGHTS

I'm going insane
don't have much time
turbulance, trouble
going on in my mind.
I've got to turn off
so I can't feel the pain.
As I look beyond their people disguise
and see their thoughts, fears and lies
that they think they need to survive
It makes me wonder
does anyone exist
who thinks like this?
I think not
but who am I?

*Maria Isabel Lopez*
*Brooklyn, New York*

# TOGETHER BLACK WOMAN

My me of life is very rubato
even though your tutti lighs
above my staff line,

My body is black and my blackness
is of being woman.My lips
are silver,too good to be kissed
by the stench of your breath,

My fingernails are gold;too bad
you can't have them.

My me is black,bold and lovely.
My soul is a whole 'nother
smoke that's too heavy to touch.

My B.O.D.Y. is all your silver
and gold mixed.Too fine,too fine,
too fine for fools of copper
and [- - - -].My me is bad,too
heavy,too sly,too much me,
too much black,too much of the
together black woman for
your black [- - -] to touch.

*Raven Lifsey*
*New York, New York*

# THE LAST HOWL GOODBYE

i dont usually write letters to magazines but there are hallucinations living in my room full of red lines and grinning darkness—all over speedlimit signs and around turned out overhead ceiling burned out lights and glaring by the curtains and beaded door . . . watching me in my sexmachine fantasy trying-to-sleep bed at night

i dont usually write to institutions like this but people are dying around me inside of me and because of me people i dont even know but actually i love them with all my heart; people dying even though one hundred years ago unborn grandparents were told they were children of the universe no less than the trees and stars and now even the stars are dying and trees chopped down and children die of old age at first birthday parties in the middle of treacherous birthdaysong dirge

i dont usually take these steps out of the crowd of pedestrian middle-americans but i read in the papers that someone cried on christmas and a thousand silverblue trees dropped ornaments breaking pretty presents right and left in tribute and i heard on the radio that in a damp prison my brother lost his hope and silently sat down to four grey walls forgetting his joy at we shall overcome three *ams* of long ago

and i walked down the pavement and fiercely stared at anonymity of each house a reproduction and none a home and castles for the sky only nobody walking the street but me i'm nobody and nobody shaking my hand

and i sat right down to this message

i dont usually write letters to brick walls but this is my last howl goodbye and i made it good to eat made it blue ink and a steno pad and you can
read and read and never
quite see more than these words

i don't usually write letters to anybody but
i wanted to make sure you turn off that light when i go

. . . whoever you are

*Laura Sky Brown*
*Sedona, Arizona*

# The Male Protagonist

## PART III

*Erin Connell*
*Carbondale, Colorado*

# THE ENCOUNTER

He was walking along the dirt road of the reservation when he saw her. He noticed her because of the way she was sitting—with her back very rigid and her head held high. She was old, very old—just how old one could never tell with Indians. She looked as if she were molded from the clay hut in front of which she sat.

He walked over and stood in front of her and, though he towered over her, he felt small and inadequate, as if he were standing before an awesome, ageless monument. And when he spoke to her, he felt as if he had sinned, shattering a holy silence.

She lifted her head slightly. She really didn't look at him, but into the very depth of his soul; then through him as if she were disgusted at what she saw. Her cold bottomless black eyes never blinked nor changed expression. He felt foolish and meek, a scolded child. He thought he would leave but he felt held to her, searching.

Her silver hair was brittle and straight like straw and twisted into braids that reached into her lap. She smelled of leather and wood smoke, like a dog after a run in the woods. He felt such a sudden urge to see her, to know her thoughts, that he all but shook all over.

She seemed to sense his anxiety, for her eyes lost their chill and became warm black velvet. Her cracked, chapped lips revealed a hint of a smile. Her weather-beaten bronze face folded into a thousand small wrinkles that started at the eyes and crept to the temples and forehead. And in that moment, the barrier of a thousand years, a thousand lifetimes crumbled, and headlong emotions washed away memories of the bloody wars, the killing, the hatred. On a little bench by a shabby clay hut, two heritages were united in understanding.

*Patricia Steenburgh*
*Johnstown, New York*

# A SUSPENSION

As he sauntered in to the meeting room, the 15 male members of the School Board shook their heads disapprovingly at his plaid slacks. Along with these trousers, he wore his usual brightly colored shirt, subdued by a wool sweater. On his feet, he wore the currently popular style of leather boots.

The members of the School Board noted that he stood about six feet and three inches tall. He was slender and his unwrinkled, sun-bronzed face and blue eyes provided a handsome contrast to his curly blond hair and sideburns. His congenial grin revealed snow-white teeth. Wisps of an aromatic after-shave lotion reached their noses. (It was probably "English Leather.")

After the School Board had inspected him, they glanced down at their notes for background information. Here they learned that he taught English, and was a Vietnam veteran although he was only 26 years old. They also learned that the demands for his English classes always topped the demands for classes taught by any other teacher. Between classes, his students encircled him.

The background report went so far as to print personal habits and interests. One such item was that he refrained from smoking during school. He was also the most zealous supporter of the school teams, cheering the loudest and longest at every game. Another item was that he was anti-Nixon. The final item, however, surpassed all the others. It reported his leisure-time activities! It said he spent his winter week-ends in the mountains and his summers in Hawaii.

Meanwhile, he had been conducting his own little inspection, first of the meeting room, then of the School Board members themselves. The room was actually a dark and dismal hall. Its windows were shrouded with the conventional type of drab draperies. The floor, which was covered with linoleum squares, reminded him of a skating rink since it was so polished and smooth.

Next, he turned his attention to the School Board. As he peered through the blue-tinged cloud which hung over the length of the mirror-like mahogany table, he counted fifteen members. He noticed that at each seat there was an ashtray which .was precisely aligned with the edge of the table. To him the members of the School Board resembled a series of portraits with the true artists hiding behind the pictures, preferring to remain anonymous.

They looked so much alike. They all wore black suits, white shirts, dark-colored ties, and black shoes. (Come to think of it, they looked like penguins!) Every one of them had a brief case on the floor beside his feet. They were all middle-aged and wore gold wrist watches.

His thoughts were interrupted, however, by the voice of the president of the School Board. Directing his attention to the president, he noticed his features. This gentleman had a pinched nose and tight lips. His beady black eyes peered over the wire-rimmed glasses and his hair was slicked straight back.

Then the teacher listened to what the president was saying: ". . . and we therefore demand an explanation for your irresponsible actions on last New Year's Eve."

The teacher then replied, "Sir, although I consider actions in my leisure time my own business, I will attempt to explain the incident to you. Being a young bachelor, I wanted to welcome the new year with my girl friend. So, we went to a party at her friend's house. There I had a few beers—just enough to get me fuzzy. As you know, Sir, most people "celebrate" the coming of the new year. Most people look forward to the future. To continue, I had expected to sleep at my buddy's house across the street, while my girl friend planned to stay at the house where the party was held. When I knocked at my buddy's door, however, nobody answered. The windows were dark and the door was locked. My buddy had forgotten me and so I had no alternative but to drive home. On the return trip, the policeman must have noticed how slowly I was driving because I was stopped and arrested for drunken driving."

The president then said, "I am afraid that the fact still remains that you were driving under the influence of an alcoholic beverage and you were arrested."

Upon this, the School Board pressed about the president's chair and the buzz of their discussion filled the room. Finally, they reached a decision. Addressing the teacher he said, "We have decided to suspend you as a teacher in this city on the grounds that you are a bad influence on the students."

The teacher accepted their decision with resignation. He turned on his heel and left the room. He realized suddenly that this hearing was hypocritical. The only difference between himself and the members of the School Board was that they carried on all their murky affairs behind the doors of their homes. His only fault was that he had been too dumb to realize this before.

*Cynthia Grant*
*Westbrook, Maine*

# RESCUE

They had quit bombing, for a while at least, so I sat with my hands under my armpits trying to sleep. But the cold was so intense that if I had fallen asleep it might have been for good. My body was in constant vibration, because of fright, because of hatred, because of loneliness, because of coldness. Everything around me was a haze of smoke, fog, and sleet. And any minute there would be bombing. The sky would light up, then darken, light up, then darken.

My mind was a blank and my body numb. I didn't know if I were alive or dead. My best buddy lay scattered throughout the jungle. There were wounded lying around me, also many dead.

All of a sudden I heard the roaring of engines. I thought it was the enemy coming back, but it was American helicopters coming for the wounded and for records of the dead. I was so happy, I would be rescued from this living hell. Now I could go home to my wife and little boy.

A group of corpsmen stepped down from the helicopters. They looked as if they were walking into a graveyard. First there was a corpsman who went around with a clip board and wrote the name of each dead or wounded. After he wrote down what was on each one's dog tags, he shouted "Michael Dubey, Dead," or "John Brown, Wounded." Then a group of corpsmen either put the wounded into a helicopter or put the dead into graves.

"Let's put 'em six to a grave. We've lost so many this time, there isn't time to bury them separately."

"Hey, there's my buddy, Marcferd. We enlisted the same day."

"I think we have 'em all."

"No, there's one over there." The corpsman walked over to me, picked up my dog tags, and yelled, "George Smith, Dead."

*No, no, this can't be. I'm alive. Don't go away, I'm alive. I'm not dead. Please! I'm not dead.*

"OK, boys, let's put him in the grave with those two boys there, and let's close 'em up. Let's get on with this burial ceremony, we haven't got all day!"

Please don't put that dirt on me. Don't! NO!

"Our Father who art in Heaven . . ."

*Vicky Gutzman*
*Glendale, Arizona*

# THE LONER

He was just walking along, that Halloween night. His Ma told him to go to Tony's place and get some pizza for dinner. So he went. He didn't ask any questions. He didn't bother anybody. He just went.

It was about a mile to Tony's and he'd been walking a while when he heard footsteps behind him. He didn't pay any attention, though. That's the way he was. The kids at school stayed away from him. They said he was "strange" because he minded his own business. He didn't like to waste his time talking about girls and pot and stuff. People said he "looked like a mean one," too. But he couldn't help that, so he just remained a loner.

After a while, the footsteps began to recede, and just for a moment, he thought he heard whispering. Probably just some Halloween pranksters, he thought, out to make trouble for someone.

About half-way to Tony's, he was beginning to get hungry, so he decided to jog a little and get there faster. But when he started to jog, the footsteps slap, slap, slapped right along behind him; and when he slowed down to rest, the footsteps slowed, too. When he began to near Tony's, he thought he heard the footsteps start to gain. Very little, but enough. He began to be but was not yet frightened. Well, . . . maybe a little nervous . . . just maybe. Still, it was close to midnight, Tony's would be closing soon, so he ran.

Finally, he reached the tiny alley behind Tony's. It was then that he heard the footsteps bearing down on him. Seconds later there were cold hands on his face and eyes; hands and feet beating him down, down into the ground.

A year has come and gone since that Halloween night. He lies now in the cold city mortuary, classified under "unidentified."

His family knows he is there, but they are afraid to leave their run-down apartment to come and identify him. For they know that when they do, the same thing that happened to him will eventually happen to them; know that if they do, they will eventually lie with him in the mortuary, no one daring to come and identify them.

*Connie Burkett*
*Phoenix, Arizona*

# ONE LESS DAY TO FIGHT

Today was a day no different from any other for Cat. His street buddies had come to call him that, for he had a reputation as the "scavenger who wouldn't give in." From the moment he awoke on one of his familiar doorsteps, he began to hunt for the bare necessities of life: food from a garbage can, water from a puddle, or if it were a successful day, maybe even a sock or a shoe.

But what his hungry eyes desired most were the metal coins, which would make that wonderful clinking noise on those rare days when he had more than one. For it was with these that he could buy the juice of his life and the fuel of his existence.

Though Cat's dependence on alcohol was great, and his love for it even greater, he knew that it had brought about his present way of life, a life in which each day, each hour and each minute was a struggle of survival. And Cat knew that in the streets, just as anywhere else, "survival of the fittest" was the law. With this knowledge, and a lust for life, Cat gained his reputation and earned his title.

Cat was an intelligent man, for he did what he had to do and he did it well. His mind was always alert, and never did an opportunity escape his scheming mind.

One bright but nippy November day, Cat was leaning comfortably against the wall, one of his many familiar resting stations. He was cold, tired and hungry, but still he was comfortable, for these were feelings he had grown accustomed to. But still they were there gnawing endlessly at him.

In the distance Cat spotted two well-dressed

and distinguished-looking gentlemen. As they drew closer to Cat, he noticed they continued their conversation, but eyed him suspiciously. This was one of those opportunities Cat was not going to let pass by. He approached them slowly, and politely interrupted their conversation with, "Excuse me." They stopped, perhaps out of fear or just sheer politeness.

The two gentlemen were astonished at the words which flowed from this inhuman looking creature. For Cat's appeal was given with genuine feeling and a quality which really reached them. He spoke not as a bum off the street, but as a person with needs. And when Cat spoke, you listened.

But his words couldn't compensate for his appearance. When Cat had finished, they shoved him aside and walked quickly and briskly away. He was left staring after them—watching as their figures grew smaller and smaller and finally disappeared. And with them, they took a little more from Cat's will to live, and determination to fight to maintain his life. For they represented success, and he, failure. But each of his defeats (some days many and others few) was hard on Cat. However, out of necessity, he had learned to live with them.

As after all his failures, Cat's mind raced. Life was too challenging for him. Where would his next meal come from? Where would he sleep that night? How would he bear the cold? And when would this fierce cycle end? But if there were men like those two who lacked compassion but had obtained success, who could he blame but himself? Was life worth living?

As would any man who has some respect for his life, Cat knew that however difficult, it was worth fighting to sustain. So he returned to his wall and leaned his weary body against it.

*Wendy Liss*
*Yonkers, New York*

# FOG AND THE BABY: A Children's Story

I remember a story about a man William and his lady Jane. They lived in a stone cottage by the ocean in Scotland (foggy Scotland, and fog is really the whole and only point of the story). In the place where William and Jane lived, the fog sat on the ocean, it sat on the rocks, it sat on the hills, it sat on the birds, it sat on the stone cottage, it sat on top of everything and inside of everything.

In the mornings, William, standing at his window, could not tell the gray of the ocean from the gray of the sky, and he could not tell the gray of the sky from the gray stones of his own cottage. William's hair was always damp and he thought sometimes that his eyes were no longer the blue they used to be. He loved his Jane dearly, but her skin was gray as the stones and her hair hung in little wet strings about her face. William remembered how white her skin used to be (when his eyes were very blue), and he was almost always sad.

Now, maybe you are asking (and you must be asking because we all forget our own human nature): Why did this William and this Jane, who loved each other dearly and must have been somewhat young in years, why did they stay in such a horrible, horrible place? I don't really know. Perhaps they had forgotten the things they used to know. Or perhaps the fog had gotten inside their heads and clouded up the thoughts that might someday have led them away.

I think they talked about it once, sitting at their dinner table, eating soup that wouldn't let them see to the bottoms of their bowls.

"William," said Jane, "why don't we move away?"

"Where to?" asked William.

"I don't know. Just away."

"We can't," said William.

"Why not?"

"We just can't."

"I guess you're right," said Jane.

But, anyway, William loved Jane dearly, and they both worked together on the sheep's wool that they sold in town, and he never let her feel alone in the fog.

One year, in September, William and Jane had a baby in their heads, and in May Jane could feel it swelling hugely inside of her. William and Jane were very happy about the baby, but they were unhappy too.

"I'm very happy about the baby," said William one day.

"Oh, me too," said Jane.

"But, one thing," William said.

"Oh?" asked Jane. She knew what he was going to say.

"We live here in this foggy gray place by the gray ocean. The sky is always gray overhead," said William.

"Even the house is gray," Jane prompted him. "And the food we eat, the chairs and tables, the clothes we wear. Everything is gray."

"Even us," said William sadly.

"Even us," said Jane.

"Well, then." William shuffled his feet and twirled his thumbs. "What about the baby? Won't the baby be gray and foggy too?"

"Oh, William!" Jane burst into tears.

William took hold of her hand, and he wished

he hadn't brought the whole thing up in the first place.

"Jane, don't cry," he said. "Maybe the baby won't be gray after all. Maybe it will be beautiful and fresh and white. Probably, in fact."

It was no good. Jane was grayer than ever.

"Even if it is," she sobbed, "even if the baby is the purest pure color you ever saw, no time will pass at all before it turns as gray as everything else in this horrible, horrible place."

"But, we won't let it!" said William.

"What can we do?" asked Jane. "What is going to happen will happen, and we can't stop it."

William sighed and stared at his thumbs. "I suppose you're right," he said. "Besides, the baby's inside you, not me."

"I can feel already. It's going to be gray," said Jane. She put her head down on the table where they both were sitting and cried into her arms.

William sat and sighed and, as I remember the story, there were tears in his own once-blue gray eyes. And every day passed the same way as they waited for the baby to be born. Every morning, Jane and William rose out of bed and ate oatmeal from oatmeal-colored bowls. Jane was very big now with the child, and William had to help her from the chair when they finished eating. After breakfast, William went outside to find the dusty sheep, and Jane followed with her broom, sweeping the fog from the stone porch as she watched him fade in and out of sight on the dully heathered hills above the sea.

Every night, after a dinner of potato soup, Jane and William sat quietly in the cottage and looked at the floor. They could not look at one another because they would rather see stone gray than their own gray, and they did not want to think about the baby. Jane was sorry for William because she remembered his blue eyes, and William was sorry for Jane because he remembered her beautiful white skin.

One morning, Jane felt the baby sweetly pushing her from the inside, and that night, it lay free and new and asleep in the crib beside her bed. Its fingers were curled into little balls and its dark wrinkly face every once in a while gave a little twitch about the eyes. William stood over it and looked at Jane.

"Well, it's a girl," he said. "It's very nice."

"It's gray," said Jane sadly.

"I know," said William. "But that's OK. It's still a very nice baby."

"It's gray," said Jane.

The baby woke up suddenly and began to cry. It cried a loud, high, healthy cry, and William and Jane were not worried because they knew that it was just a baby sound and nothing to get worried about. William picked the baby up and laid it down beside Jane on the bed. Jane held it cradled against her arm and rocked it back and forth until the crying turned into little quiet happy gurgles that made the parents laugh.

"She's gray," laughed Jane half-sadly.

"She's all gray and foggy," laughed William, not-so-sadly.

The baby gurgled and wrapped one small hand around her mother's thumb. She held the stubby fingers of the other hand up in front of her own face and chuckled happily at the marvelous Scotland fogginess of them. William and Jane chuckled too.

"Foggy gray baby," chuckled Jane.

"Foggy muggy gray baby," chuckled William.

"Foggy muggy buggy baby gray," laughed Jane.

"Foggy muggy buggy foggy foggy dew gray baby," shouted William.

"Oh, yes!" shouted Jane.

And William went to the window, opened it, and the air rushed into the room. He breathed and breathed and chuckled, and down below the stone cottage the white froth of the ocean waves was giggling as it pounded on the rocks.

*Mary E. Wood*
*Los Angeles, California*

# THE MOUNTAINS

It was going to be a hot day; he knew already, even though it was only seven-thirty in the morning. Yesterday had been hot, and the day before that, and a week before that. The chilly mountain air only helped a little; usually, it was so cold in July that he wore his hiking pants and heavier jacket. But this summer in his cabin in the sierras he felt different. There was something strange about the land . . . It had an ominous lull about it, distinguishable only to someone who knew the country well, as he did. The sun seemed to shine more brightly—the sky seemed a more radiant blue—the clouds drifted more peacefully along—the waters seemed clearer, fresher, more pure than ever before; the mountains seemed even stronger and more majestic than usual. Ah, yes, the mountains . . . those beautiful, huge, respected monstrosities of nature which always did have a certain magnetism for him. Ever since he was old enough to creep around, the mountains seemed to watch over him, to make sure he didn't go anywhere he shouldn't. At night, their whispering trees sang a soft lullaby until he was fast asleep. During the day, they were still there—never moving, always watching over him—until the day he had to leave them.

He still remembered that day; he was only six years old when the man came to talk to his mother. They talked and she seemed to agree readily, saying something about how they could stay with Aunt Helen in the village and come home on vacations. Peeking shyly from around the corner of the four-room log cabin, he realized he was going to be forced to leave his mountains—for awhile, at least. His mother thanked the man, and he got on his fine horse and carefully made his way back down the steep mountain trail. Mother seemed to float around, singing gaily, glad at the chance to send her only son to school. "Oh, wouldn't daddy be proud of his little man if he were only alive today!" she thought happily. He knew, even then, how both his parents were brought up by wealthy families and were very well-educated. His father had had a successful law firm in the East, but had decided he liked the free, natural life rather than the stuffy, business world. They agreed to build a home in the mountains and live there, where he was born. However, the hard mountain life in the early 1900's was too much for his father. He died of a heart attack when his son was only two years old, leaving his family the property and cabin in the mountains, along with a substantial sum of money from his business back East. The growing up had been hard at first, but his mother had done quite well; he was extremely intelligent for six years old and the brightest in all his classes at the village school. And the mountains were always there—they, too, had taught him. He could climb as swiftly and as quietly as any mountain goat; he could track animals with great accuracy, hunt, fish, and follow trails at thirteen with the precision of an age-old mountain tracker.

As time went on and he grew older, he knew he'd have to leave the mountains he loved for some time. He went to Harvard in 1923 to follow in his father's judicial footsteps, and he also set up a fairly successful law office in the tiny Nevada village, although considerably smaller than his father's in the East. Each summer he'd go alone to visit his beloved mountains, since his mother was at this time living permanently with Aunt Helen, and carry on any business from his private office there. Each winter he'd go back down to the quiet village and write when he had the time; he loved to express himself on paper—to tell the stories of his brothers, the mountains. They inspired him; they whispered ideas, and he wrote them. A few of his stories were published in the village newspaper and in small, unknown magazines, which gave him additional funds. He led a quiet life, at peace with himself and his paternal mountains. He never found time for marriage; he never allowed a relationship to build very far, mainly because he never met a woman who could share his experiences and understand his closeness with the mountains. Women tried to keep him in the village or persuade him to move East, so they could live in the elegance they desired. He had no close friends, either—no human ones, at least. The mountains were his friends; they were all he needed or wanted.

As he grew even older, the villagers began to whisper after he passed, to eye him queerly, to stop talking suddenly as he approached. His business subsided, he withdrew into himself even more, and gradually he became more and more distant. After his mother's death, he decided to retreat to his mountain sanctuary permanently, where he'd be in the midst of tranquility and undisturbed contentment. Once a month, winter or summer, he'd come down to the village for supplies, living as a hermit and being talked about by the misunderstanding, misjudging townspeople. When winter storms confined him to his cabin and prevented his getting supplies, the mountains cared for him. They sent stray animals to his doorstep for food, and they provided the endless snow he melted for water. Firewood was no problem; he always stored adequately for a complete, harsh winter. The mountains had taught him to be prepared always for the unexpected. They were excellent teachers.

Spring in the Sierras was an experience in itself. The aging, natural beauties seemed to come alive all over again after their long slumber; they radiated green, natural life, inspiration, and an immense feeling of superiority and power. He enjoyed his life; he didn't care what people thought of him. He knew what true happiness was—they didn't.

As he stood there that morning in his short, white pants, his flannel work-shirt, light jacket, and hiking boots, with his shaggy white hair blowing in the caressing breeze, he decided it would be a good day for carrying out his "reminiscing plan." He was going to hike all day, re-exploring the ancient caves he had discovered as an inquisitive youngster, reevaluating the streams, plants, rocks, sky, and animals he had thought so much about as a boy. At sixty-eight, it would take him a little longer than it used to, but the mountains had been good to him. From them, he had learned to care for his body the way the mountains cared for themselves; he was in fine physical condition for a man of his age.

By eight o'clock, he was ready. He carried a knapsack on his back filled with food he would need, and a canteen of sparkling, cold spring water was slung on his shoulder. Following a straight path from his front stoop, he soon found the slightly worn trail he remembered so well. It was growing over with velvety, soft moss, which offered a quiet, green carpet for his feet. He progressed silently and quickly, glancing every now and then at the huge, majestic trees and places where he heard twigs snapping under the weight of an occasional deer or leaves rustling where an unseen snake slithered along. He felt young again; it was going to be a good day, he thought. If only the eerie stillness would break! It left a strange feeling inside him—something he couldn't understand. But the day was warm, it looked especially good to him, and he was going to make the best of it.

After two hours had passed, he began to tire a little. He stopped at a very special place, one he remembered as giving him ideas, the silence in which he could think, the view about which he could contemplate and write. It was nothing more than a cluster of aging rocks which had stampeded down the mountain long ago during an avalanche. They were solidly in place, and here he dropped the now heavy back-pack and sat down to rest. He ate some cold sandwiches, wiping the sweat from his brow, and drank long from the blessed canteen. When he had replenished his strength and energy, he stood on a protruding boulder and looked around. Straight ahead loomed a small range of hills and mountains which he'd been waiting to find again. He was there; the caves in which he had allowed his imagination to run free were embedded at intervals along the sides of these mountains. The excitement of revisiting these wonders of nature where he had spent so much of his boyhood built steadily, forcing his heart to beat faster and his breathing to come quicker. He gave one last look around before setting off to reunite himself with such age-old memories; the sun was higher now and beat down upon his bare head fiercely. There was a gentle, whispering breeze, drying his moist face and carefully nudging him from his rocky pedestal. He stepped down, and leaving his knapsack on the rock pile, proceeded toward the mountains as to a secret lover not seen in a long time, slowly at first, then quicker and quicker until he was trotting along at a rapid rate. Before long, he slowed down. His breath was short, clipped, there was a pain in his chest, and he was nearly at the base of the mountains. He sat down, leaning against the soft grassy mound of earth, until his breath returned to normal. He sipped at the canteen he had refilled at the stream he had crossed, and then he was ready to continue up the sloping eruption of earth.

Halfway up, a solitary crow flew above him, circled once, and emitted a mournful, raucous cry. He looked up, startled, and his eyes followed it until it was no more than a dark speck in the sky. Nothing like that had ever happened to him before. Perhaps it was just the strange feeling he had acquired about the day itself, he mused. He shrugged it off as nothing, and soon the incident was forgotten.

He was nearly there now—the first cave was no more than fifty feet away. Soon he came to its gaping mouth, and trembling with excitement, suspense, and the arduous task of the long trip with no really good rest, he lit a long wooden match which he extracted from his pants pocket and went inside. He thought he was in better shape than this; must be the soft years spent in that hateful village! Once inside, he looked carefully around, not wanting to miss a thing. Nothing had changed, except for a pile of rocks and dirt in a corner near the entrance which hadn't been there before. Must have been a small landslide after the spring rains had loosened the soil, he surmised. The same wooden shelves were where he had nailed them in the rock as a boy. On these, he kept his treasures: an Indian arrowhead he found in the vicinity, petrified wood he had discovered embedded in the earth, flat pieces of rock with strange formations imprinted on them. He also used them for his provisions when he spent the night there in a bedroll in his teens. This cave was his favorite of all the—how many were there now?—six or seven caves he had discovered. Six, he guessed. This one was the first he had seen, it was the largest, it was shaped the best, and it was the only one he had ever slept in. It was like a second home to him; the cabin his father had built would always be his first. Being in this cave, he felt the same as he had ever since he first stepped into it—close, very close, to the mountains. He was inside them, a part of them, not a stranger on the outside looking in. The knowledge that tons and tons of rock, dirt, and grass were on top of him, yet the way Nature had formed this indentation of earth not to collapse from the weight, gave him an exhilarating feeling—as though She were helping him hold up the immense mountains.

Suddenly, his thoughts were distracted by a slight, rumbling sound which became a thunderous roar before he realized what it was. By the time his mind had fully absorbed the harsh impact of what was happening and had motivated his body, it was too late. The downpour of rock and earth was already a sheet rapidly cascading down in front of the entrance. He stepped back and tripped on a small rock. Unable to regain his balance, he fell against the back wall, striking his head. Immediately, all went black, with his ears ringing from the din as he thought of the crow's warning.

When he came to only minutes later, his eyes tried to focus on the midnight blackness. With a throbbing head, he painfully reached into his pocket and struck a match. His eyes rested on a wall straight ahead of him—a wall that had not been there before and which should not be there now. Too stunned to think about the danger at hand, he ran to the jumbled mass of rock and flung his full weight against it. It didn't budge. This wall was like a puzzle just finished—only it was put together too well. None of the pieces would loosen; it was as though a magician had welded the pieces tightly together with his magic wand. He returned to the back of the cave and sat down to catch his breath and think. Before he could collect his senses, an unpleasant odor reached his nose. Gas!

The mountains were indeed kind to him. He thanked them silently for this natural gas leakage. He knew he was the only human around for miles. No one from the village had ever come to his private domain in the mountains; any chance of rescue was instantly erased. His knapsack with food was left on the other side of the valley; it wouldn't last long anyway. His half-filled canteen wouldn't offer much help; it would just prolong the suffering. Under normal circumstances (normal! he thought) he would stay alive until either his water or his oxygen gave out. At least his thoughtful mountains had provided the painless, quick death gas offered.

He laid himself down on the powdery sand bottom of the cave nearest the gas leak. He thought of how full and rich his life had been, how beautifully close he had become to understanding himself through the mountains. A picture of his mother flashed through his mind. God, she'd been such a lovely woman! He wondered about something he'd never thought of before—death. He had lived so much every day of his life that there was no time for thoughts of death. Death had come early in his family; when his mother had died, it was a very natural occurrence, and he had the best years of his life stretching before him. After a week of mourning, his business and writing had occupied completely his thoughts and time.

He closed his eyes, and knew that that was the last time he would see his precious mountains. They had watched over him every year since he was born; they would protect him now that he was a part of them, inside Nature's womb.

*Marsha Orzech*
*West Rutland, Vermont*

# Questioning

## PART IV

*Nettie Spiwack*
*New York, New York*

## LIFE?

(flower<br>
            bird<br>
water)<br>
      air SUN<br>
clouds and stars;<br>
moons, sounds<br>
earth , time , songs:<br>
      "rain"<br>
sand People!<br>
      ((mountains))<br>
grass and streams<br>
      trees<br>
                    rocks<br>
                                    life?

*Jennifer L. Roberts*
*La Canada, California*

## ONE LAST MACHINE

The stone bridge arching over a brook,<br>
A long blue mirror with trees in its face.<br>
The smiles of silver flecks of sun.<br>
Weeping willow with her graceful arms<br>
Looking down; she whispers Nature's<br>
Private language. One the<br>
Human can't hear.<br>
One he can't destroy.<br>
The one thing man can't conquer<br>
Is himself.

*Theresa Churney*
*Wauwatosa, Wisconsin*

## TIME

Time is like varnish.
It can seal off memories,
But you can still see them.

Time can preserve memories,
But with each coat of years,
The vision grows dim and hazy.

*Cindy Keith*
*Superior, Nebraska*

## MEMORIES

*An echo still lingering*
*A time still existing*

A piece of Time dangerously existing
On a slender thread
Ready to be—
Snapped into oblivion
If not recognized by a light—
Spin between people

Fragile as Glass
More brilliant when scattered
Across the expanse of a mind
Remembered only when a ray of
Uncertain Light
Walks barefoot across a more
Uncertain soul.

*Jo Ellen Kwiatek*
*West Valley, New York*

# THE HUMAN CONDITION

The fall of 1972 was a period of enlightenment and discomforting revelation. The preceding summer, I, who consider myself a moralist in the sense that I cannot tolerate human cruelty, had reached the peak of my awareness of the atrocity of war, of Vietnam in particular. In my adolescent naivete I vehemently believed that American society was as totally outraged as myself. Unfortunately, I had not lived life so long as to fully recognize the controlling force of greed and pride on human behavior. Therefore, when I realized the import of the opinions expressed on this issue by those whom I formerly respected, I became deeply disillusioned with the human race and its hopes for the future. Inconsolable depression haunted me, accompanied by uncontrolled crying. I felt mankind was doomed to nuclear holocaust.

Compounding the problem and gloom of the above situation was my preoccupation with it to the point that my school work and all other activities began to suffer. (Heretofore I had unquestioningly devoted my existence to achieving the highest grades possible on the assumption that I would be accepted by the greatest college in the world, where I would miraculously and suddenly be infinitely happy. Having never been very happy, achieving this novel experience seemed worthwhile.) Inwardly, I berated myself and resolved to work more diligently; however, during this lull in my scholarliness I began to question my way of life. Was it worthwhile? Was I enjoying life? Unhappily, I saw my sixteen years as barren and wasted; I had feared close relationships with others and was habitually alone. I was unable to cope with other people and often would not leave the house for fear of having to communicate with someone. Once confident that I could contentedly inhabit a desert island by myself, I now buckled under the demands and pressures I imposed on myself. Thus, I was compelled to realize my inability to tolerate myself as well as others; I then included myself in my all-consuming hatred of mankind. I gained much satisfaction from wistfully contemplated thoughts of a future in an insane asylum and of suicide.

Fortunately, I came to realize that I have a duty to survive and that that survival depends on my acceptance of the human condition and the illusions that people, myself included, must live by. I will never condone greed and war, but must take a more optimistic outlook—that I can make the world better, that I can and will fight with every last ounce of conviction all that is unjust and immoral on this earth. Perhaps that is where satisfaction lies for me. Perhaps that is when I will finally respect myself. The fear looming large before me now is that death will catch me without my having accomplished much in my lifetime. I have lived for the future, DISREGARDING THE PRESENT, but what if that future never comes? Then I fear that I will die miserably wretched.

*Jane Bobko*
*Newington, Connecticut*

# GREEN DISEASE

I don't need to have money.
Because I always thought if you are
Green, it means you're sick.
It means you're really sick.
What do you think your ailment is?
Is it your stomach or your mind that is
Twisted in illness? Money and greed:
They walk hand in hand.
The more money, the more greed.
Money, Money, Money. Greed, Greed, Greed.
And this greed covers you like mold until
You spoil.
Isn't it evil to know fungus and money
Are
Green?

*Theresa Churney*
*Wauwatosa, Wisconsin*

## SONG

one day (soon)
i'm gonna give out my heart in tiny pieces
my soul will be strewn on the floor
my head will burst open
my guts will be sold for a penny or more
i'm gonna be a leading lady in the family
rock and roll band
i'm gonna sing so heavy
blues like a baby's eyes
jazz like you'll never witness
rock and rhythmic soul
you'll beg with pleasant pain for more
get on down with your
juice grass uppers and downs
i got a series comin' round
earplugs and cigarettes
take more from me, the tension won't lessen
i think i'll retire around thirty . . . . . .

*Sarah Lee Sandy*
*Charleston, West Virginia*

## HE SAID

Oh go to hell
He said.
So I did.
So
I
did.

*Sarah Lee Sandy*
*Charleston, West Virginia*

# A NIGHT POEM

Late hours of the night
bring out a part of me
that hides like a firefly
in the day.

After the sun has
long been down and the
darkness is in full exposure,
slowly something inside
begins to flicker.

Beginning faint, weak, unsteady—
Sensitivity unfolds one petal at a
time until it blossoms in the
warm security of night time.

Things do not move so fast
in the night, and love seems
so much softer and emotions
and ideas lose some of their
Inhibitions.

Late hours of the night
bring out a part of me
that outshines any midday mood—
Because in the dark, you cannot see,
and you have to depend on
Fireflies to guide the way.

*Carole Faye Rheins*
*Indianapolis, Indiana*

# BALANCE DUE

Never say, "he's not adjusting."
Adjusting is the law of living.
As no one can quite say who is sane,
(remember Einstein's theory of relativity . . .)
So each has his own adjustment,
his coping.

Unique as his thumbprint and voice waves;
—patterns of his compensations.

If life gives, then he must take.
Pressure. Release.
Boredom balances the passion.
one adjusts by ignoring. one with ulcers.
The balance is as easily met
with paranoia.

Payment must be meted out in equal but
opposite proportions,
the flavor of which is of no concern.

He who compensates with froth,
we find a straight-laced jacket for,
He with pained expressions and nerves of steel,
a briefcase.

the Last, when life offers no more options
—remains the same.

Then the cold shroud tips the scale
for the final weighing
and leaves only
the funeral expense.

*Penny D. Sackett*
*Omaha, Nebraska*

## CHILD OF THE MOUNTAINS

As a child, at a rather early age, I began to keep a diary, although the events recorded were of no particular significance, other than that of childhood memorabilia. I was supposedly then at my most vibrant stage of innocence, knowing nothing of the prejudices, problems, and pressures that belonged, exclusively, to me. I had lived in a sheltered atmosphere all my life, and as the obstructions and problems became too much for me to grasp, my perspective outlook on life changed completely. Upon growing older, and as I was introduced to new sights and sounds, the diary was set aside and forgotten. I suppose everyone, at some time or another, goes through a period of trying to find out who he or she is and where he or she is going. I was no exception. I believed in identification, and that to grasp this connection with reality and some other plausible object, I needed to know that somewhere, someplace, someone else was in the same situation I was experiencing.

Upon learning to "find" myself, I began writing poetry and short stories. Under cover of flowery phrases and studied paragraphs, I could then reveal myself without fear of someone guessing the real truth. What I was writing then, was actually not an attempt to project a part of my true self into the works, but instead, instilling a series of tired metaphors and over-worked cliches. What I wanted most for myself was for other people to see me as I *wished* to be seen.

It is often not easy to live in a community far removed from large cities and towns. After living in an area for so long, you tend to overlook its achievements and magnify its shortcomings. Yet, as people, as human beings who continually seek to expand our minds into all branches of understanding, there is a tendency in all of us to place upon others the handicaps of labels. And to know everyone, to understand each person with deep, unprejudiced knowledge, would take a lifetime.

My roots, however firm, are fastened deep in this country of mine. It is not so much nostalgia, though, as an abiding love I feel for my state. Perhaps she has taught me something—a pleasure in living, or else a strong fierce pride that makes me proud to be who I am—a child of the mountains. Gentle mother, healer of all ills, she cradles me in her depths of Appalachia. West Virginia is my home. She is endowed and marked by high rolling hills and mountains, unexpected leveled fields and meadows, and punctuated by silver streams and rivers.

Yet, when I venture from the recess of my boundaries, I come upon a totally new degree of prejudices. "They" say we are a proud people; a fierce people best left untouched. We are brought together under one expanse of blue sky, neatly packaged, wrapped and tagged.

I have never seen the bright lights of big cities, or experienced heady feelings of excitement in all the rush of its days. Many would say I was nothing more than an outsider looking in. Is it so easy to compare differences? One is encouraged to be "mod," "with-it," the total sophisticate, without becoming "hung-up." But isn't that really what we're doing? Becoming so engrossed in petty situations, we forget why true value was lost in the first place?

However, I am not free from criticism. My disabilities go deeper than drawling my r's, or going barefoot. I criticize myself as I write this, for fear I know too little, or am dramatizing the situation too much.

What of people? Has there ever been any attempt to analyze what they feel? In a minute observation of faces—in each—there lies a certain story. In many, there are lines furrowed deep. They are often silent, impassive, and stony—then, it becomes hard to read between the lines. However, if a story must be told, the best place to search is in the eyes of the children: dejected, forlorn, or happy-carefree; each emotion reaches out to grip you—unlike the eyes of adults, who seem devoid of emotion.

I live in the season of dreams. I am a child of the future. Looking back, I see the changes that have come upon us all. No longer a child; but not quite an adult. It is all new to me, and as I grope and reach to understand, I am aware of others.

Bring us new ideas, cultures and life-styles, and do not estimate our abilities by the boundaries of our weaknesses; but allow us the dignity to preserve ourselves as whole human-beings—persons who are truly free.

*Renee Stauffer*
*Princeton, West Virginia*

## INERTIA

There are no answers; only questions.
There are no colors; only arbitrary illuminations.
There is no reality; only a universe of illusions.
        Galaxies of eternal truths waltz
        in their predetermined elliptical orbits.
                There is no escape
        from the known.

There is no intelligence; only an electronic labyrinth.
There is no depth; only one dimension exists.
        Your length depends merely on how long
        it takes you to get
                from there to here.
STOP IT.

*Dianne Marie Piché*
*Hicksville, New York*

## CHESS

A child is born to its parents,
To the world,
Unknowingly, to life.

P–K3

The child opens eyes to love,
To hate,
To confusion between the two.

KB–QB4

The child stands, wobbles,
And is pushed down.
It is made to crawl first.

Q–KR5

The child reads a book,
Understands, hopes, cries.
Why is the book closed?

QN–QB3

The child grows up, unwilling,
Unwanting,
Tired and old at 18.

Q x P CHECK

A war breaks out. A fear breaks out.
A child fights, a child dies.
The skies weep over a new-dug grave.

CHECKMATE

*Mary Ann Schaefer*
*Omaha, Nebraska*

# MY LIFE

My life is like a maze,
I don't know which way to turn,
Or how to escape its windings.

If I make a wrong turn,
I cannot go back for the past
Is sealed behind a locked door.

At the end, there awaits
Only one exit—death.

Only God knows how long
It will take me to complete
The winding, turning maze of life.

*Cindy Keith*
*Superior, Nebraska*

# PEACE

Across the dark, gray, cold, hard sand,
God and the devil walked hand in hand.

*Deborah Dotson*
*Queens, New York*

# A SMALL BATTLE

It was a small battle;
We suffered only light casualties—
21 dead.
Their deaths affected only a few:
42 parents
and
21 wives or girlfriends
and 42 children
and 21 sisters or brothers
and 631 friends.
Their deaths affected only a few.
Only 757.
It was a small battle.
We suffered only light casualties;
We won the battle.
Or did we?

*Sharon Kramer*
*Brooklyn, New York*

# PREDICAMENT OF THE DEPRESSED

The mind has withered
Like dried straw
Crackled and crumbled
In shallow tones
Resounding
Where once only thoughts
Breathed
Now caught in a
Broken tangle
They die before
They can speak . . .
Humanity left mute
Wails silently for
Crucifixion.

*Jo Ellen Kwiatek*
*West Valley, New York*

# FREEZE-DRIED DHARMA

instant karma's gonna get you, gonna knock you off your feet, hendrix everybody get together try to love one another right now and where has my baby gone—down to the heartbreak hotel and don't you need somebody to love, it's your thing do what you want to do you know we're running just as fast as we can, but here come ol' flat top he come movin up slowly an you got to pay your dues if you want to sing the blues janis an don't you ache just like a woman, watch it now a hard rain's gonna fall an if you want to be a rock an roll star just listen now to what i say . . . an here's mama joan, she came in through the bathroom window an she's just gonna sing a little song for all the lonely people—hey jude, don't be afraid, i'm just looking through a glass onion an what would you do if i sang out of tune, today is my birthday we're gonna have a good time an me an bobby mcgee got our chips cashed in an we're truckin down to hear carlos and sly an joni an peter an we're not gonna take it an we all got together for some dancin in the streets and mcguinnn says you all look alike an wow, man, did you hear? morrison died———amid a sea of madness

Hey, now, that's all right, i'll sing rainbows all over your blues. an janis died, but don't let it bring you down, its only castles burning, yes, om—on with the show we'll sing this song all to gether an share a little joke with the world an what do you know here HE comes!!

if not for you
your clothes are dirty but your hands are
clean and

you're the best thing that we've ever seen
all you got to do is act naturally?
you've let us down, man, where have you
been, father of
night, father of day, father who taketh the
darkness away?
don't think twice, it's all right.
an baby, you're a rich man, baby, you're a
rich man, baby,
you're a rich man, too.

*Carol Packer*
*Cedarhurst, New York*

# JOURNAL, 18 SEPTEMBER 1972: VERDUN

In the gray month of March it stood out like a cut in white flesh: painful, alone, a shadow in the sun; Verdun.

I was not quite seven years old at the time. Skinny, awkward, solemn, and shivering inside my winter coat, Verdun struck me as a place where all the dead had done their dying. It was a place as damp, and as gray as the March earth and sky.

The pale gray-green woods stood about the town, hiding the secrets of the past. They were a filtered curtain around rusted guns, and the fifty-year dead. The woods hid the land mines, and secreted their instantaneous death. Only the signs posted about told one of the forest's past.

The deep trenches still scar the moist earth, but the scar on human life is deeper still; the ones that died became a lost generation, and the ones who lived, the maimed generation.

Even after the guns were laid down, the bleakness remained to wrap the town in a fog. Even after the guns stopped blasting away at the town, the silence itself became stronger.

It has been ten years now, but I can still remember Verdun. I can feel Verdun, the cold the rain, the sky, and the rusting instruments of war, all broken pieces of a terrible mosaic upon the earth.

*Maria Lisa Hansen*
*La Jolla, California*

# CONFLICT OF WILLS

A small pass in the Jura Mountains of France, Verdun Way is merely a stretch of mountainous road used by perhaps twelve people in one year. The time was the seventeenth century. This is the story of two men who met on Verdun Way one hot and dusty afternoon, and how their "Conflict of Wills" decided the future of the people of Verdun Way, France, and the world.

The people of the nearby village of Vallorbe said that Verdun Way was formed by one glacier which came from the heavens and did not begin to melt until it landed one hundred yards from Verdun Way, forming Lake Neuchatel. The people of one village named this sacred glacier "water-gate." Those who used the Verdun Way were farmers who wanted to water their cattle and horses. It was believed that if a farmer brought his cattle and horses to water in Lake Neuchatel, he would have a profitable year. If he bathed where the cattle and horses had drawn water, it would mean that under all the rocks that he stepped on for the next month, there would be two gold pieces left to each of his children.

One day, in the Village of Morez, a farmer was getting ready to bring his cattle and horses to water in Lake Neuchatel. In another town named St. Claude, a farmer was readying his cattle and horses to take them to Lake Neuchatel. Both farmers left from their different towns on the same day. After one half day on the road, the farmer from Morez decided to stop and rest. The farmer from St. Claude remained on his route. In a matter of three hours, the man from Morez was approaching a fork in the road. Up ahead he could see the farmer from St. Claude. As they neared the fork in the road, neither was sure of the correct road to take. They did not speak to one another. The farmer from St. Claude decided to take the road that the other farmer was coming from, thinking that he had already been to Lake Neuchatel. The farmer from Morez decided to take the road that the farmer from St. Claude was coming from, thinking that he had already been to Lake Neuchatel. As the two passed each other, the cattle that belonged to the farmer from St. Claude spoke to their master. They said, "Master Paix, the road to water is the road not taken." The cattle of the farmer from Morez spoke. They said "Master Honneur, the road to water is the road not taken." "Peace" walked with "Honor" and "Honor" walked with "Peace" to the water of Lake Neuchatel. To this very day, "Peace" and "Honor" have never been seen again on earth.

The knowledgeable people of the nearby village said that perhaps the great glacier "watergate" had come down from the skies and taken "Peace" and "Honor" away. The people said that "Peace" and "Honor" would not return until the children of the earth had overturned every rock and harvested all the gold pieces.

*Mary K. Nolan*
*Schuylerville, New York*

# TO BE AN AARDVARK

To be an Aardvark is not the most unusual thing in the world. However, most people do not think that Aardvarks are everyday, common matters. The truth is that once you've seen one Aardvark, you've actually seen them all. Only, you usually don't know if you are going to see an Aardvark before you see it, and you don't know if you are seeing an Aardvark when you see it. But, most important of all, you don't know if you've seen an Aardvark after you've seen it. Or, did you see it at all?

That brings us to the question all of you have been waiting to ask. What is an Aardvark? Well, if you want to know the truth with no artificial anything, I'll tell you. I don't know. Now, to some of you, this may seem a little strange, because, if I did not state it before, I am an Aardvark. But no matter. I mean, don't you agree that just because I am an Aardvark, all six-week-old flies are Aardvarks?

My name is Eric.

My fellow Aardvarks are a ten-year-old girl, a two-year-old cub, and a grasshopper.

Now, what do you think an Aardvark is?

*Linda Blum*
*New York, New York*

# Relationships

## PART V

*Erin Connell*
*Carbondale, Colorado*

## BEQUEATHAL

Leave

a token
of yourself
for others—
a look, a gesture,
a thought.
Let it bloom
in the world
and find a home
in the
mind
of others.

*Sharona Levy*
*Brooklyn, New York*

## PLEASE

Don't shut us out,
Reach us,
Don't stand in doubt,
Trust us,
Don't simply scold,
Teach us,
Don't be so cold,
Need us!

*Cynthia Akin*
*Wahoo, Nebraska*

# WOODEN BOXES

Sitting in my wooden box
I feel safe and secure.
No more can you look down upon me.
No longer will I see your icy stares.
Yes I feel safe now.
To let you know me.
Is too great a risk.
To get close to you
Is a chance I must never take,
So I'll remain hidden.
I've seen the way you look at me.
From your high pedestals way above.
There is no difference, north or south,
You're still white and I black.
It is irrelevant that I'm living
In your house.
'Cause I live in my own world,
My black world.
Please don't try and talk to me.
'Cause I'll only walk away.
How do you dare say there is "equality"
When you look at me
As an ignorant nigger, so inferior.
And you, the great white race
So clever, so superior.
You can change the laws
And free the slaves.

But you can't change the ideas
Embedded in your minds.
I see no reason to believe or even hope
That this will ever change.

The rules are clear to me,
And I must play your game.
So don't pretend to be my friend,
Or talk about equal rights,
Until you've lived as I have,
A nigger, in a white man's world.
Don't you see,
Black is black,
And white is white
And we're as different,
As day is to night.
So now you know the reason why
I'll remain hidden,
Isolated from your world,
Sitting in my wooden box.

*Cathy Smith*
*Huntington, New York*

# A MOMENT'S CARING

I saw her standing on the corner
waiting for the light to change.
There was a look of worry in her
eyes. Did her son have the flu? Her
husband had run away? Maybe she
was dying and didn't know how to tell
her family. Or maybe she had no family.
Was she wondering where she'd get
the money to pay for a new car? Or did
she even have enough to buy her next
meal? Did her feet hurt from wearing
such old shoes? I wondered if she
had stolen that coat.

And then the light changed.

*Sheri Huddleston*
*Casa Grande, Arizona*

# MARIAN

Endings are so sad.
The top of a candy mountain.
New interests.
Lost memories.
File cabinets of my mind.

If we win—Yea!
If we lose—Cry?
Either way
I'll never see you again.
Lost?
Should I file you under lucky,
        or unlucky?
Or should I refrain from
filing?

Will you leave me??
Like everything else in life?
Or will you stay?
A custom-made slot appears,
and you are filed
into
Me.

*Heidi Libner*
*Muskegon, Michigan*

# THREE YEARS (OR IS IT FOUR?)

Of patient hope
  cartwheels for joy
    daydreams (technicolor)
      long days, short nights
        twisted meanings
          lilacs and pale pink roses
            Camelot
              holding hands (+)
                Valentine surprises
                  grubby blue jeans
                    the Big Slipper

And private jokes and people jokes
  "hitting the pave"
    late night telephone calls
      hockey games
        59¢ pizza and Old Mill
          the El Roco, Buxton
            love letters
              etc.

*Kathy Breiland*
*Buxton, North Dakota*

# BUT YOU DIDN'T

Remember the time you lent me your car and I dented it?
I thought you'd kill me . . . . .
But you didn't.

Remember the time I forgot to tell you the dance was
formal, and you came in jeans?
I thought you'd hate me . . . . .
But you didn't.

Remember the times I'd flirt with
other boys just to make you jealous, and
you were?
I thought you'd drop me . . . . .
But you didn't.

There were plenty of things you did to put up with me,
to keep me happy, to love me, and there are
so many things I wanted to tell
you when you returned from
Vietnam . . . . .
But you didn't.

*Merrill Glass*
*Ellenville, New York*

# FLEXAGON

*From the Diary of Lisa Covey*

Monday, April 16, 1973

Wow, I'm dead tired from moving and fixing up. The house is neat! It seems real large; 4 rooms, *and* a bathroom. So Mom will sleep with me, instead of in the kitchen. It will almost seem lonely without 3 other people in the room with me, but only Mom. *Also* there's an attic. We will have to fix it up a real lot, but when we do, it will be like a fun, work, play, study room.

In one way I *kind* of wish we hadn't moved. I'll bet there won't be a guidance counselor in this tiny school as neat as Adrienne Jaffe was. She told me a lot about people in general, like that I'm going to have to work real hard to get someplace. Mom married when she was 16, because she was pregnant (with me, I guess). She doesn't know anything. She managed to get a job (when I was 10, old enough to take care of the others) cleaning. Her mother was like that too, and she went crazy. I wonder if Mom will.

Anyway, Adrienne was real neat. She convinced me to learn to be something, even if only a mother, to be a *good* one. Make *myself* happy, even if I don't make any money. And by the time I've really fulfilled my needs, *not* by getting pregnant either, I'll probably be able to do something useful. I'll be a good person.

She also told me stuff like why people don't like me, which was real interesting. People on welfare are considered just bums who aren't trying. I also am too dark, and people call me *nigger*. My clothes are too weird. I've decided to not try by wearing makeup, and stuff, to make other people like me. I'm going to *wear* weird clothes, and *be* dark and ugly and like myself. Sometime somebody will like me, and in the meantime Mom, Michael, Sheila, Alex, Carla, Gerome, and Mona will like me. All of them sort-of hated me while I was wearing make-up. Mom thought I was trying to be above her. Michael, Alex, and Gerome sneered at me, Mona hated how I looked and acted, and Sheila and Carla sort-of envied me. They are only 12 and 9 but they wanted to wear make-up too. Mom said *no*, I could spend my money how I liked, but they couldn't.

Now that I think about it, I don't know how Sheila and Carla are going to turn out—they are stupid. I think they're going to catch a man as soon as possible. They'll be good at it, too. I hope there'll be somebody like Adrienne for them, but I don't think it would help. They are so sure that they're right.

Mona is real neat. She likes me a real lot, and we get along well. I've been helping her with her work this year. I don't think she'll stay back, even though all of us so far have stayed back in first; Sheila also in third. I think Carla may stay back this year, the same as Sheila. I've been trying to help them sometimes, but they call me stuck-up, and don't let me help unless I just give them answers. I *really* don't want to do that. It doesn't help them any.

Well, I've got to iron some clothes for school tomorrow. Tomorrow's the first day, and I might as well have something vaguely decent to wear.

*From the Diary of Letitia Allison*

Wednesday, April 18, 1973

Ellen says that somebody new has come to school while I've been absent. She lives near me.

Her name is Lisa Covey, and she's ugly, and wears hand-me-downs. I wish, for a change, somebody *nice* would move here. All of the kids here are horrible. Ellen is barely passable.

I guess Ellen's typical: giggly, interested in being popular, normal. The "normal" means that everybody is the same, never thinks anything that anybody might disagree with, or rather, everybody acts at all times as if they would really like to be ex*actly* like the others.

I'm going to try and get well fast, and go to school tomorrow. I want to make up my work before the weekend. I also would like to meet this new kid. I'd like a friend: Boolaberry is nice, but horses don't talk back: riding, reading, writing don't really take the place of a friend either. I *wish* she were nice, but it doesn't sound as if she is. So I'm going to get some sleep. Good-night.

*From the Diary of Lisa Covey*

Thursday, April 19, 1973

I'm going to fix up the attic in this house. It's dusty, and it needs cleaning, painting, and a couple of lights; it only has one window at each end. We also need tables and chairs, junk like that. I'll have to make the money for it, because Mom doesn't make much cleaning, and welfare doesn't add enough to that to spare any. Michael and I are going to see how much we can make babysitting, mowing lawns, etc. I have the number of somebody who needs a babysitter: Mrs. Polis. Also there's a teacher who sometimes needs help with inside and outside work. Between us we ought to be able to make some money.

Something weird happened today, which is depressing me, that I've been avoiding talking about, but I'm going to: This girl, Letitia, nicknamed Tish, I think, had been absent. She's overweight, and has long, red hair. She looks nicish. But she acted real nasty. She started asking me questions in a nasty way. Maybe she was trying to get to know me, but I doubt it. She had enough friends already. Also, people just don't act like that if they want to get to know somebody.

She was interesting in classes. She talked a real lot. The kids seemed bored. The teachers kind of like her, and kind of resented her. It just depressed me that someone who seemed so nice should be so horrible. Oh well.

I think I'll call that Mrs. Polis now, talk to Mona and Michael, go for a walk, or something. Take my mind off this horrible school and on to nice people and ideas.

*From the Diary of Letitia Allison*

Thursday, April 19, 1973

I saw Lisa today. First of all, she isn't ugly. I actually think she has something that if she were nice I'd call beauty. She *fits*. She has dark frizzy hair, dark eyes, and she has dark enough skin to really look good. She's thin.

Anyway, I tried to talk to her during lunch. She was walking away from the people on the playground. I went over to say hello. I figured that she might be nice, and I'd know fastest if I talked to her. Right?

I told her that I'd been absent, that I'd wanted to meet her, and was she Lisa? She coldly informed me that she was *not* Lee-sa, but Lee-za. Then I said, "Oh, why does everybody call you Lee-sa?" "They didn't listen when I told them." I asked her how she liked this school. She said, "I suppose you'll hate me if I tell you that I can't stand it." "No, because I can't stand it most of the time either."

I asked her where her family was from, and why they had moved here. She named some rather large city, I've forgotten what, and then she said: "I don't know why we moved here." Then all of a sudden she got *really* angry, and said "Yes, I do: welfare decided it would be cheaper to buy us this house, and then they would own it instead of having to pay us the rent for it."

She looked at me as if to say: "Now you hate me; I hate you too." And then she walked off. I can't really figure it out. I *don't* hate her for being on welfare: if you can't make it, you can't make it. I think that the family is pretty large. I don't understand why she hates *me* so much; she just acted horrible when I started coming near her. I've got to clean Boolaberry's stall now and shut up.

*From the Diary of Lisa Covey*

Friday, April 20, 1973

Tish and I are friends. I'm going to write it all down, as much like it happened as possible. We were talking about ecology. Everybody was for it. Then Tish said, "This class, this whole school, probably including me, is hypocritical about two things: one is ecology. If everybody is for it then why is this school yard so messy? The other thing isn't connected with this, and I'm not going to bother mentioning it." The next period was a study hall that I have with her in it. I was real curious about what the other thing was, especially since after she said that she kind of glanced over at me like, "Well, *you* must know what the other one is, don't you? And I don't want to embarrass you by saying it now."

So I asked her what the other one was. She said, "Well, everybody is against racism, or racist people, but do you know how they treat blacks, Puerto Ricans, or any other minority groups? Well, even take you. Somebody told me that you were ugly. As far as I can see the *only* reason is that you have a dark complexion, and have dark frizzy hair. So you look like a 'P.R.' or a 'nigger.' " Then she added, "I can't think of anything else that this town is *really* hypocritical about." I said "Do you think that you are hypocritical in the same ways?" She smiled, shrugged, and said, "I hope not. Let's put it this way: I don't litter, or drop trash on the ground. And I *do* like the way you look. I know that my reaction to blacks is *different*, unless I know them well, but I hope it is not negative." I said, "Oh," and went back to my seat.

A while later I heard the teacher asking for somebody named Leessa (Lisa, "s" sound). I looked up. He was looking at *me*. So I said, "Do you mean *me*?" "Yes, of course, there aren't any other Leessa's in this class, are there?" Tish said, "There aren't *any* Leessa's in this class." The teacher glanced at her. A kid hissed, "He didn't ask you, Tish." The teacher said (to Tish), "What do you mean?" Tish: "Her name is Leezza, and this school seems not to be willing to recognize that fact." The teacher didn't really say anything.

During the lunch recess I saw her and went over to her to ask her if she thought everybody would start calling me "Leezza." She said: "By Monday morning two things will be all over the school. First that you and I are great friends; second, that your name is Leezza, and the easiest way to make me mad is to call you Leessa." Then she added: "Do you think we should let them be correct, or make them incorrect?" I realized that she meant, "Are we friends?" Well, we are.

*From the Diary of Letitia Allison*

Friday, April 20, 1973

I told Mr. Moreland today about Lisa's name. I think I may have also complimented her looks. Anyway, she took it as my way of telling her that I didn't hate her, because she came over to talk to me during lunch recess. I told her that everybody would think that we were friends because of what I had said to Mr. Moreland, and should we satisfy them? She said "yes" without really saying it. A while later she said "You *didn't* hate me for being on welfare, or for being dark, or for my clothes, did you?" "No." "So I just *thought* you hated me." "Yeah, and I thought *you* hated *me*." She smiled, "Well, I don't and you're neat, and beautiful." I felt like hugging her, and saying, "Thanks for everything. I love you."

I've been thinking about people today: they are rather interesting. The only inanimate object that they remind me of is a hexaflexagon. A hexaflexagon is a strip of paper folded into a shape that looks hexagonal, but if you "flex" it (fold it in a certain way) you can find many different sides. Sometimes you only find a few of the sides, and sometimes it is not being flexed and it just is hexagonal, so you never know what the other sides are like. I know how to make a hexa-hexaflexagon (six different faces). And I know a flexagon that is not hexagonal in shape, and I don't know how many sides Lisa has. Also, *I* am a flexagon too. I suppose everybody is, but most people only see one side of most other people; maybe even people like Ellen have another side.

Well, Lisa's coming over tomorrow, and in the meantime, I'm going to bed. I never thought anyone thought I was beautiful before. It'll be something to go to sleep on.

*From the Diary of Lisa Covey*

Sunday, April 22, 1973

Happy, love, beautiful, friend. All of the words have a superficial idea connected with them as well as a real one. Charlie Brown and "Happiness is . . ." "Love is . . . (having a boyfriend who likes your make-up?)" Miss America, who is beautiful? (who is *pretty*, and doesn't have enough *substance* to be beautiful). Friends that giggle together, get in fights over *nothing*, talk about *nothing*. Well, maybe about what they really think, but they sure don't "really think" much.

I don't mind all that anymore. I *am* happy. Happiness is having a beautiful friend, who thinks you're beautiful, who loves you for being you. Excuse the superficial words. You can't right the world in a day.

*Jennifer Rice*
*Hatfield, Massachusetts*

# WITH HOOF, PAD, AND PAW

How sad, indeed, when one's house is not a home; and yet, sadder still when one's house is not really one's own house. To what, you ask, am I referring? Simply to those creatures of instinct and habit, who have no powers of thought or reasoning. Actually, I am awaiting the day when the three of them: the "Red Devil," the "Gray Ghost," and the "White Shadow," will band together and evict us from our own—pardon me—their own house.

The "Red Devil" is perhaps lowest in the ring of conspirators. Her outside connections are perhaps too far outside to exert a great influence over our daily lives. Nevertheless, the ensuing conversation is heard frequently.

"Hi Mom. I'm home."

"Go give your horse some carrots. She's not feeling well. I noticed she wasn't eating." Some greeting.

"Why should she be? Any more alfalfa and she'd burst."

"She's not fat!"

"So that's why I couldn't get the cinch fastened yesterday."

The "Gray Ghost" is the newest addition to our family. She arrived a few weeks before Christmas —some Christmas present. Oh, she loves my dad, and tolerates my mom, but she made her opinion of me quite clear the first night we had her. I'll admit she was rather scared and lonely, but that was no excuse for her sinking her feline teeth into my thumb when the dog rushed by my feet. After all, he wasn't going to hurt her. Some gratitude after being rescued from the cold and damp! (Even if my mother still swears it was at least 80° out.)

She has another way of expressing her violent emotions towards me. I happen to be an avid collector of bric-a-brac, and she happens to be the clumsiest ox I've ever seen. The other night she was on my nightstand, and what a mess she was making.

"Get off that nightstand! Do you hear me? Get off!" At this point I was violent, but rather hemmed in by stacks of homework.

"Why don't you hit her instead of just yelling at her?" asked my father later.

"And break something myself?"

The oldest, most established member of the syndicate is a dignified, four-year-old cock-a-poo. Let me assure you that these qualities make for a strange combination. His rule has slightly diminished since the coming of the Ghost, but he still reigns. He is also, ahem, shall we say, well fed. His main disability is vision. You see, he mistakes several commonplace things for trees and fire hydrants—things like bedroom furniture, living room furniture, den furniture . . . in fact, you name it, and he thinks it's a tire.

Well, there they are as I've described them—the real owners of our house, even if their signatures aren't on the contract. After all, we wouldn't want to mislead the bank. They might think we were some kind of commune.

*Pat Walsh*
*Scottsdale, Arizona*

## WE WERE SUCH GREAT FRIENDS

We were such great friends
and such great liars
hating the sudden silences
seeking smiles around us
inseparable because we feared
becoming separated into
ourselves.
We two were never more than
butterflies;
we felt the longing of words unexpressed
and let it slip from us
thinking it would come again
but it never did.

*Dina Grussgott*
*Brooklyn, New York*

## TO VANITY FAIR AND FRIENDS:

Bam! Biff! Pow! Bang!
I can be Batman, too!
I could strike out with my sharp tongue
        cut you to shreds
        if I so pleased

But I don't
I would rather flee on my favorite unicorn
        protected by my magic shield
        to a very, very quiet castle

And ignore you

*Kathy Breiland*
*Buxton, North Dakota*

# FOR YOU, IT IS EASY

For you it is easy to say nothing.
You are like the lawn in my yard—
    grass does not speak.
There is a fence around your being—
    not tall and having no paint.
You bear only weed—you are not
    cared for.
You are dead from being walked
    upon—never loved.

Not long in the past are the days
    when you were bright.
You were not so forgotten then.
There was much inside—shared with
    all those around you.
But you say nothing and now so easily.

*Laura Mainhood*
*Torrance, California*

# YOU SEEM TO FORGET

you seem to forget day to day,
first lover of mine that i ever loved,
how hard you leaned on me
the last time.
we made it mystical.
still in public
i am an accessory only to
approve your down to the
earth. review your performance
after waiting through
rehearsing and staging
and recuperating and now
backstage—another fan.
after the production
you will call me, or so
you said the last time.
i caught you just as you
left for the theater.
you only need me when i
insist.
your turn.
meanwhile i pretend to leave town.

*Kathie Merrill*
*Plainfield, Vermont*

# LAURA AND NAN SING IN WASHINGTON PARK ON MEMORIAL DAY . . .

we sat in the long grass
stretching marbled thighs into the sun
our voices
joyous
gaining strength
with each pair of eyes and
two guitars
we climbed
wine in hand
to a climax of green
shade
caring for nothing
but the sound
of our own music
imposing thigh
melting into knee
and rounded
calf
ending
in the isolation
of five toes

lawrence ferlinghetti
i know your friend
he's beautiful and like
a small boy
which is nice
however i could
take being called
princess
for only so long

*Nan Peterson*
*Portland, Oregon*

## SHE IS SOMEONE

She is someone
But I don't know her
Better than he
She's got to be—
Who is she?
I've never met one like her
But she's there
in my dreams all day.

He? Well he's different
than I
In fact, we have little to share
other than "love."
What is love? To me
To him
it seems something different
But love affects me very little any more
I used to live for love.

*Reiko Obata*
*San Diego, California*

## HYBRID

Mama's white
her lover, Black
(They probably forget
in the dark)
I'm neither
and hate them both.

*Reiko Obata*
*San Diego, California*

# THE MOTHER

I'm a friend of a sister
of a son-in-law
of a mother
But most of all the mother
who ended her own life
in a trailer camp
    getting drunk with sleeping pills and tequilla
    watching a baseball game
with a man with machismo
who didn't save her
or ever find the keys
because she hid them away.
She had it all figured out this time.
She was unsuccessful before
the man found her like a drowned rat
and she told us desperately—I was almost . . .
She was a lonely woman
    never without a drink
    too far ahead of time
    and too old she thought
But she never will know what Liberation means
She must have truly given up hope
risking the chance that her life might have improved.

*Reiko Obata*
*San Diego, California*

## INCANTATIONS FOR A WOULD-BE MAN

aha—you shall soon stand trial
all because of me
all on my account
(all at my expense, come to think of it).

    and all the men behind
    all the meat counters
    instill a bubbling terror in me now.
    and suspicion is rampant in the street.

and what was it you wanted?
i'm curious in spite of myself.
a feeling of power, perhaps?
(aha—you should have known it wouldn't last.)
or was it just a good lay?
i can see how that may have been a problem
what with your wife's stomach
sticking out to here.
must have been partly your fault,
though.
proof of your manhood, then?
what's manhood, anyway?
power? victory? a hairy chest?
oh, you poor sucker.
i bet you don't even know.

    and all the men behind
    all the meat counters
    will go home tonight, to their wives.
    and you? rampant in the street?

aha—you shall soon stand trial.
i can hear the song your wife will sing
to that child that will be
all that's left of you:

"your would-be father will not be home tonight,
my would-be husband will not be home.
go to sleep a little, while i think a little.
i thought i wanted the right thing
but what can you mean to me now?
now that what i wanted is obsolete . . .
go to sleep a little, while i think a little,
go to sleep a little—"

and all the men behind
all the meat counters
will instill a bubbling terror in her
and suspicion will be rampant in her arms.

and she may scream:
"what was it you wanted, anyway?"
and she may scream and scream and
scream at me.
we lose, she and i,
having given you what you wanted.
or was it just
what you were taught to want?
oh, you poor sucker.
i bet you don't even know.

and all the men behind
all the meat counters
will go home tonight.
and you?

you lose, you would-be manfatherhusband.

*Kathie Merrill*
*Plainfield, Vermont*

# CONFUSION: A PRECARIOUS BALANCE

My friend has liked him for a long time; as a teenager becoming a young woman, it has seemed like an eternity of separate moments bound together by her longing for him. He does not appear to see her or to really grasp her need for him. Oh, he knows she has a "crush" on him, but what appears to him as just a crush is actually a feeling that is crushing her soul. She lives tottering between a dream world in which her wishes are fulfilled and a feeling of vague emptiness because of her need for him to care for her and the lack of the deep relationship she craves.

Reasoning will do no good; all she knows is what she feels, however deep and utterly real it is, but she does not understand that she is living and reaching for something that may never be attained. If she leans too much further, she may lose her precarious balance and fall. Then who will be there to help her up? And so she goes on hoping, and no one can truly understand this thing that has her clutched in its hand. Not even her.

I sit and listen to my friend as she tries to explain. I try to comprehend what she tells me, but I, not possessing her soul, can't really feel it. The beauty of her individuality is overshadowed by the confusion of her situation.

I watch as she traces a heart in the condensation on the car window and draws a small question mark within it. "Help me," she silently screams and then wipes away the evidence of her struggle from a cold window. Where the fog was wiped from the glass, I look through to a deep, tall group of green trees on a hill, and I wonder, "Why can't she wipe the confusion from her mind and see the beauty of life and really feel?"

*Karen Obinger*
*Portland, Oregon*

# SAND IS A USELESS NECESSITY

Sand is a useless necessity. It wedges between toes, and beach blankets, and tunafish sandwiches. It tumbles out of hair and ears and sheets for days and days. But it is necessary, because without it, there would be nothing to hold up the ocean. And besides, without sand, I might never have had an excuse to start talking to him.

I met him here, on this beach, perhaps right on this very spot. He was walking laboriously, because he was carrying what seemed to be a bucket full of sand. He huffed and puffed and every so often he put the bucket down, very gingerly and wiped the sweat from his brow. When he stopped again, it was next to my blanket. The umbrella hid him from view, but I saw his feet and then the bucket came down heavily. He was walking towards the ocean.

"Are you going to put all the sand on the beach back into the ocean?" I asked. (How else do you start up a conversation with a pair of feet and a bucket?) A head appeared.

"What?"

"Are you going to put all the sand on the beach back into the ocean?"

"I don't understand." He really looked puzzled. How dense! "The bucket. Sand. You know." I pointed to the bucket, ready to drop the whole subject, indeed very thankful to be able to drop the whole subject.

"He grinned. He had a beautiful smile. "Naw! Just this load."

"What's so important about this load? There is a lot of sand on this beach. I'll bet there's a very important patch you overlooked."

He laughed. He had a beautiful laugh too. "I don't think so, look!" He dropped to his knees and we peered into the bucket together. With the sides of his hands, he parted the sand, and about fifty clams appeared.

"Wow! Did you find all of them?"

"Yes." He seemed proud of himself.

"What for? Don't tell me you just come to the beach to look for clams so you can put them back into the ocean again!"

"He looked me straight in the eye and said, "I used to come to the beach for that reason (his eyes twinkled) but I guess I have a better reason to come now." His eyes were brown. And I know you won't believe this, but they were beautiful too.

After that first day, we spent every day together. At dawn until midnight we were together, at the beach or the movies or at lovers' leap (a romantic name given to a three foot ledge overlooking crabgrass and tumbleweeds). I drank more malts that summer, saw more Westerns at the movies and gazed up at the stars and that yellow moon more often than at any other time in my life that I could remember. He used to play with my hair late at night on lovers' leap, and tell me how he loved me and would never leave me. He loved to let his fingers get tangled up in my hair; he loved to hold it to his face and smell its sweetness. And I loved him to do it.

One day, we were sitting on my blanket watching the waves. It was a hot day. The beach was crowded. And it felt good to be alive. He turned to me.

"I have something for you," he said.

"Oh you do? It better not be a clam."

"No!" He laughed and played with my hair.

"Look! Here!" From his beach bag he pulled out a little white cardboard box. My heart skipped a few beats. He handed it to me. I took it. "Well, open it. See what it is already!"

I lifted the cover off of the box. His eyes shone with excitement. It was gorgeous. "Oh gosh! It's *lovely*!" I lifted the pearl necklace out of the cotton by its silver chain. "It must have cost a fortune! You shouldn't have. But I'm glad you did!" He laughed and hugged me. I put it on. "Do you like it?" He nodded his head. "Do you really like it on me?"

"I love it on you."

"And I love you." I leaned over and kissed him. That night we watched the moon. It was big and fat and yellow. It was a horrid and sickly yellow color. He held me tight, but the moon still glared down on us. "Let's go inside," I said.

That was the last time I ever saw him. He left for home the next day. There was a note in my mailbox. A little sliver of a white note folded in half waiting for me. "I'll be back," it said. That was all, and "Wait for me." So I cried and cried and held the note to my heart and waited for him to come back. As the note said, I waited. He never came back.

So, here I am standing on the same beach, maybe even on the same spot where we first met, only a whole winter and a whole summer later. I missed him. I miss him still. I took the necklace off last week and threw it into the ocean. Today, I am getting a haircut. It is summer and I want to be cool. Long hair is a bother. And besides, I don't need it to keep me warm on cold, clear nights. Because I never go out to look at the moon anymore.

*Julia Ann Ward*
*Beverly Hills, California*

## IN MEMORY (*an epitaph*)

Always I have strived to keep
Protected some of the innocence of the
Child—to be a little surprised,
A little awed, and a little vulnerable
to life's love-sorrow.
And so the woman lived
Hand-in-hand with the child—
In life; and for eternity carved of stone
in memory.

*Susan Radke*
*Omaha, Nebraska*

# SCRIPT FOR A LIFE ON EARTH

I'm sorry.

As if two words
Could mean what I meant.
I've spent my life saying them.
I blunder, and I don't mean to
But once the mistake is made
There it sits
Waiting for amnesty.

I had no plan to hurt your feelings
No intention of insulting you
No matter what it was I said or did.

I am a fool. I make fool's mistakes
Blind and unknowing, though,
Honestly, I didn't mean it. Whatever it was.
Must I swallow everything I am for your forgiveness?

I'm sorry.

*Laurie Walker*
*Syracuse, New York*

# ON THIS DAY

Mend a quarrel, search out a forgotten friend,
dismiss a suspicion and replace it with trust,
write a letter to someone you miss,
encourage a youth who has lost faith,
keep a promise,
forget an old grudge,
examine your demands and vow to reduce them,
fight for a principle, express your gratitude,
overcome an old fear,
take two minutes to appreciate the beauty of nature,
tell someone you love him,
tell him again
                    and again
                    and again—

*Mindy Buckman*
*Yonkers, New York*

# QUESTIONS AND ANSWERS AT HOME

1. "Will you unload Goldie #1," (the dishwasher)?
   No I can't—you know I'm class prez.
2. "How about cleaning out the car?"
   You know I *have to* put my eye-makeup on, and I don't have time.
3. "Could you please run over the floor with the vacuum?"
   Aw Maw, we have to go downtown now—I need some gum.
4. "Please feed the dogs, Rhonda."
   I have to practice my trumpet first.
5. "Would you please clean the bathroom Lanelle?"
   Mom! I've got Algebra to do. Then I gotta practice cheering . . .
6. "Could you do up these few pans?"
   I'm tired—I think I'll go to bed.
7. "David, the garbage is crawling!"
   Forget it!
8. "Laurie, will you please sweep the basement floor?"
   Yea—you bet. You had to spoil my supper by bringing that up.
9. "How about doing some raking?"
   Not now. I gotta shoot baskets.
10. "Have you ever considered making your bed?"
    You don't want me to miss the bus do you?

11. "We need the garage straightened . . ."
Why? It'll just get messy again.
12. "It's 11 o'clock, don't you think it's about time to hit the sack?"
Goll—I have to wash my hair.
13. "The dogs could use a bath."
You don't want me to get fleas, do you?

*Laurie B. Lommen*
*Buxton, North Dakota*

# HOW TO STAY OFF A DIET

1. To forget about eating, eat a lot.
2. Fill your stomach with a considerable amount of food.
3. Banish all lettuce, low-cal dressing and TAB.
4. Think of how the thin people suffer in the cold winter.
5. Remind yourself how comfortable you sit at hard chair events.
6. Have you tried dancing with hard knees and bony elbows attacking you from all sides?
7. Avoid health spas and organic restaurants at all times.
8. Use a lot of grease and oil.
9. Buy a franchise from McDonald's.
10. Think fat!

*Laurie B. Lommen*
*Buxton, North Dakota*

# PRECIOUS WORTHLESSNESS

Today he left me. I had sensed that it would happen. That familiar restlessness had surged up to the high water mark, and he could not allow it to flood his life. He had made promises and pledges ad infinitum, but, they were always broken. To him it was like promising never to blink again. It just couldn't be helped.

Since we lived on the coast of Massachusetts, the temptation was always before him. The pounding surf, the screeching gulls and the briny air did not represent the beach to him; rather they represented the open sea and adventures. Of course, when the winter whaling season came, the temptation became too great. Whaling was his greatest love. So, when I came to this realization, I simply packed his sea bag, gave him a hot breakfast, and watched his silhouette become a speck on the endless seascape.

The last whaling expedition had continued for two months and I had anxiously awaited his return. In my frantic loneliness, I had strolled back and forth along the walks, unfortunately named the "widow walks," looking for all the world like a lone sentinel guarding his treasure. As I searched the horizon on these walks, my mind returned to the days when he was courting me. I could still remember that first church social we had attended together. I felt radiant when he came after me, yet, he looked so uncomfortable. He kept clearing his throat. Then I thought about how worthless those memories were to anyone else, and yet how precious they were to me. But, if he never returned, these same memories would seem painful and become worthless to me, too. Then, I checked the horizon again. I didn't want those precious memories we had shared to become worthless. The sight that greeted my eyes, however, immediately calmed my fears. The white sails of his whaling ship were creeping toward the shore. He was safe!

Now, I must go through this agony once again. I only hope that the memories so precious to me now will remain that way when this new whaling expedition is over.

*Cynthia Grant*
*Westbrook, Maine*

# THAT WAS MY HUSBAND, THE KING

"Call the knights!" roared the King. "Sound the trumpets! The enemy has attacked our cities and killed our people. Call to arms!"

That was my husband, the King. I am Queen. The worst had come at last. For so long, we had been at peace and our people were prosperous. Now, it was the end, this was the great battle we had all been waiting for. It was a fight to the finish.

The knights had come to counsel with my husband while the priests consoled the pages and ladies of the court. My own bishop was with me trying to give me words of comfort.

"You of gentle nature may yet win," spoke my high bishop.

I did not know what he meant nor did I care. All that interested me at that time was the protection of my husband. In my country, if the King was killed, there would be none to rule or keep the peace. I pleaded with my husband until he consented to let me ride into battle with him.

"Call to arms. Mount the horses!" All was ready. It had begun.

The scene of the battle was a large, grassless plain. Would this be where I would spend my last moments? It could not be! I would fight to keep myself, my husband and my country alive! Two pages, one from either side, met in the middle of the field and exchanged slips of paper. Both said the same thing, "To the death!"

Out of an age old custom we allowed them to make the first advance.

"Amor vincit omnia," I whispered to my beloved. And to the bishops who were always by his side I said, "Guard him well. He is our lifeblood."

Thus I rode out to battle, for the strength of the fighting had reached me. With a fury, equaled only by the most seasoned knights, I slashed my way to the very heart of the battle. Swords were clanging, blood was flowing, my knights were dying left and right. My sword sang out its death tune and cleft straight through bone. With a thousand deaths taking place, the terrible bloodshed was evident on my side. My bishop was right. The love I had for my people and my husband had come through. Suddenly I stumbled and fell! Poised above me was an enemy sword. The end!

I gave one last backward glance at my husband. He was cornered back against the edge of the battle field, surrounded by the enemy. His bishops were trying vainly to protect him, as all his knights were dead or dying. The bishops' robes were splattered with blood. I saw now that it was hopeless. We had lost.

"Amor vincit omnia, my love," I whispered, though I knew he couldn't hear me. "Goodbye sweet husband, goodbye sweet life . . . . . . . . . ."

"That was fun. Let's set them up and play another game, David. Darn you, you always beat me. Gee, a chess game is so challenging. Almost like a real battle."

"Call the knights!" roared the King. "Sound the trumpets! The enemy has attacked our cities and killed our people. Call to arms!"

That was my husband, the King. I am Queen . . . . .

*Katherine Diane Smith*
*Peoria, Arizona*

# Walk Tall, Daughter

## PART VI

*Nettie Spiwack*
*New York, New York*

# FOR THE DAUGHTER I MAY SOMEDAY HAVE

Walk tall, daughter.
You are young, and your choices
Are as open as your brother's.
There will be no picket parades
And militant campaigns for you;
Liberation is a thing of the soul
And bears no relation to laws passed
Or battles won.
We will have succeeded only if
From our bittersweet choices,
You are born with what we fought to attain.
Daughter, I give you pride.

*Ellen Gray*
*Tolland, Connecticut*

## W.L.

Women's Liberation
something to bitch about
yeah, we're all a bunch of bitches
don't you see that's why we're complaining?

*Reiko Obata*
*San Diego, California*

## I AM A BITCH

I am a bitch
Which isn't something to be proud of
However I have my reasons
I didn't just all of a sudden become bitchy
I used to be quiet
People even called me shy
Maybe because I've held it all in for too many years.

*Reiko Obata*
*San Diego, California*

## SISTERS

Sisters,
we've got to come together.
Our men are putting us down
without our even noticing
We've got to get off the feminine trick
Men set up for us
So they could be higher-stronger-superior.
Come down off your pedestals
Show them you can open the door
   To FREEDOM

*Reiko Obata*
*San Diego, California*

## [----] YOU!

Does that say anything to you?
Maybe I've finally gotten through to you
the anger and bitterness
that I've hidden
even from myself.
It was buried inside behind all the hurt
I've felt being a woman.
Behind my soft and restrained voice
there was always a thought screaming
   to be let free.

*Reiko Obata*
*San Diego, California*

# WOMAN TO MAN

"I, Woman,
give birth to new life."
"But without me, Man,
it is impossible."
"Ah, but it is within me
that the fetus grows.
It is my blood that
carries food to it.
I, Woman, can give life
And
I can now choose:
When to give birth . . .
Whom I want born."

*Arlene Fraas*
*New York, New York*

# ASIAN WOMEN AND WOMEN'S LIBERATION

If you are a white woman, you are oppressed, and if you are a Third World male, you are oppressed, and if you are a white male, you might also be oppressed, but if you are a *Third World Woman* you face a double oppression. You are kept down in life because 1) you are a woman and 2) you are part of the Third World people (people of color). Oppression comes in several forms. Asian women face a special type of oppression and one of the severest.

All women are servants to men; however, the Asian woman is stereotyped as the perfect servant for men. A perfect servant obeys her master, is pretty, cooks good food, is quiet, doesn't complain, and is neat and clean. And so you have the stereotype of the Asian woman (at least the Chinese and Japanese women). Most Asian females try to live up to this stereotype, consciously or not, not because they like it, but because they are expected to by their parents, teachers, and by all males and non-Asian peoples in general.

Think of an Asian woman—already you probably have pictured a beautiful, exotic young woman with silky long black hair with a (sexy) smile on her face. This is what you see on television with all the commercials about Japan Air Lines, Oriental foods, etc. Think about this. There's a commercial on T.V. advertising some shampoo that makes your hair smooth and silky and they've got you looking at the back of this Asian girl. The commercial goes on for about a minute all the while showing her beautiful long black hair and not once do you ever see her face. And why not? Her hair is beautiful. Men like long hair. And men also like big blue eyes and large breasts. She has small eyes that are "slanted" and her breasts are small. These are the characteristics of Asian women that are least appealing to men. Since the Asian female finds herself ashamed and trying desperately to get accepted, she resorts to taping her eyelids (with scotch-tape) so that she won't have double-folds and wears extra-padded bras or uses silicone to enlarge her breasts. Deep inside, she wishes that she were white.

In elementary school, she remembers being called "Fat Jap" and "Chink" and feeling very different from her white friends. School taught her that men were better, that Amerika was good and white was good. She had no choice but to believe all of this. She believed herself to be "one of them" (white). Of course, she didn't want to be different. All of that "Oriental" stuff wasn't really her. Admittedly, she was Asian but she didn't really feel Asian, she felt "like everyone else." Asian was something foreign—something separate from herself . . .

As a young girl, her parents teach her well the role she is to play in later life. She sees a living example every day—her mother, constantly reminding her of what she is to be—a home-loving wife/servant. Her mother teaches her "duties" such as cooking, sewing, cleaning, and caring for her man. While the roles of daughters of other ethnic backgrounds are not so rigid, the Asian American female's role is well established and is forced upon her early in life. If she is so unfortunate as to have brothers, she gets little help from them in her household chores. In fact, she must take care of them too! After all, they also are being trained—for manhood. They soon understand that they are protectors and providers and that women are "made to serve them."

When the Asian girl reaches high school and the age where Amerikan society accepts dating, she finds that her parents do not. Many times she will have to wait until the age of eighteen or more. And when she is able to date, the boy she dates will be carefully inspected by her parents. They may or may not like her dating white boys. Long hair is usually not acceptable, and the boy's parents' occupations are important. She is seldom allowed out on school nights (because she must take care of her younger brothers and sisters and/or prepare dinner and/or clean house) and her curfew on weekends is earlier than most at her age.

The Asian woman's relationship with a man is much the same as any woman's relationship with a man except that the roles they play are more visible and more emphasized. Because of her need for outside contacts (she has been locked up in a cage all her life) and all the brainwashing she has gone through about how she needs (white) men, she will undoubtedly find love with a man. Their relationship is a teacher/pupil relationship where he teaches and she listens, he tells her what to do and she does it, he knows everything and she knows nothing, he is superior and she is inferior. He is not interested in her intellect (and sometimes neither is she) but rather her body and how she will benefit him. In other words, he is interested in himself and she will fulfill his ego.

She will act twice as passive, twice as shy, and twice as dumb (naive) as other women and she will continue this because the man likes it. And why shouldn't he? It's great to have power and status—he uses her for both.

The Asian woman hasn't become too involved with the movement for the liberation of women.

Maybe she is continuing to play her stereotype as she has been conditioned to by society, remaining uninvolved and politically indifferent. Or maybe she has a false sense of satisfaction and security or maybe, like men, she fears liberation, which proves, in fact, that she never has known true liberation.

*Reiko Obata*
*San Diego, California*

# HER LIFE WOULD BE DIFFERENT

It was a very cool evening. The light turned green and she crossed the street. She had been waiting for Michael for an hour. Ruth was nineteen now, and it was almost a year since she had moved away from her mother. Michael was her fiance. She had met him a year ago when she was traveling cross-country with a small drama troupe. He was sitting in the audience during one of her performances and said to himself, "I just got to meet that fine sister." At least, that's what he told her. As Ruth recalled it, he looked damn good. He looked wealthy too. But then if he was, what would he be doing in a little dinky theatre like that? Later he told her that he was a small time manager, but a lot of that didn't matter right then, because Michael had stood her up again. She walked a few blocks until she flagged down a cab.

The ride wasn't long, but it was long enough for her to dream about the vacation she and Michael were going to take in another month after her show closed, and Michael had wrapped up some important business transactions. As she rode up the elevator to the twenty-second floor, she thought about how much she loved her job; but she wouldn't mind giving it up to settle down with Michael. She was doing pretty well for herself. She was now doing a Broadway show. Inside her room, she kicked off her shoes, walked into the bedroom, and began to undress. The phone rang.

"I'm on my way up, baby." He didn't give her a chance to answer before he hung up. Ruth put on one of her lounging gowns. She walked through the front room, unlocked the door, and continued into the kitchen for a glass of water to take her pill. Whenever her nerves were on edge, she had to take a pill to keep her calm.

"Ruth! Hey, baby, come here." Ruth came out of the kitchen with that famous blank expression on her face.

"Listen woman," he said, "Don't go giving me those stupid-ass looks. If you have something to say, go on and say it."

"You have some nerve catching an attitude with me, Michael. I was the one who stood out there for an hour waiting for you on the corner in the cold."

"Okay, I'm sorry, all right? Now come here." He held out his arms to her.

"No, Michael. Where were you?" Michael took one look at her and she knew, she shouldn't have asked him.

"Where was I? Ha! What do you mean, where was I? Girl, you're something else. If I wanted you to know where I was, I would've told you." He sat down on the couch. She could see his body tighten with anger. She decided to calm down a little and sat down beside him.

"But don't I have the right to know where you were? After all we are getting married." That was the last thing Ruth should have said.

"You don't have the right to know nothing! Nothing! You don't own me. Look at me when I talk to you. I'm not a child that has to report his every move. You keep throwing this marriage business in my face. If you don't stop being so childish, we're not going to be married."

"Stop it!" Ruth couldn't take any more. She ran into her room and slammed the door. Michael was right behind and came in just in time to slap the bottle of pills out of her hands. "Get outta here and leave me alone," she screamed. Michael slapped her across the face, causing her to fall on the bed. She stuck her head into the pillow and cried.

"Come on baby," Michael said, turning a little soft. He sat down on the edge of the bed and lifted her by the shoulders. "Look at me," he said, lifting her chin. Ruth tried to look up but she couldn't see through her still tear-filled eyes. "I'm sorry baby. I didn't want to hit you, but I wasn't in the mood for arguing. I had a hard day."

"I didn't know baby, I . . ."

"You got to stop and think sometimes, Ruth. I have a lot of patience with you. You know I never took this much from anybody before."

"I'll try, Michael."

"You got to try harder, baby. You know I'm your man so why do you constantly worry, huh? You got me wondering why I bother with you sometimes. Of course, I want you to think about me. Hey, I should be on your mind 24 hours a day, but you got to think like a woman does, not a child. Don't make me wonder why I don't leave. Make me know why I stay." Michael lay down on the sofa and let out a sigh of relief. Ruth looked at him for a while. "Come on," he said. She bent down to kiss him lightly on his lips, but from his collar came the fragrance of perfume that wasn't hers. She dared not say anything. She just turned out the light and lay down beside him.

The sun broke through the darkness, the birds began to sing, and Bea got out of bed. She had a slight headache, but it would go away when she got some fresh air. She went about the regular routine at home before leaving for work. She hadn't seen

Ruth since she moved away. Every night she cried a little while she wrote a letter to Ruth, a letter she knew would never be answered; but still she couldn't give up.

"Hurry up, Ruth," her mother hollered from downstairs. Bea was one of those old Southern mammies, big and round and always smiling. Bea Greene was what you called a real mother. She looked right at home in the kitchen with the bacon frying on one side of her and the hominy grits bubbling on the other side while she sang the gospel with the choir on the radio. She worshipped God. You could tell by the way she was always ready to help people. "We're all God's children and we got to help each other," she would say. Look at William Greene, her husband. What did he ever think about? Money. He always had to have more money. I suppose Bea was thankful he was not lazy, though. Still, there were other considerations, like his daughter. Ruth loved her father. Why? Because she didn't really know him. In all her sixteen years, she never really knew the man who was supposed to be her father, at least not the real one. She couldn't see beyond the smiles, gifts, the assumed understanding, and the "love?". That's why it was so hard for Bea, because she could "see;" and she tried to keep it away from Ruth so as not to destroy the image she had of her father. Bea never talked about the evenings, or should I say mornings, he came in—from where? Who knew. Bea did, but she tried to overlook the liquored breath, lipstick-smudged collar, and the loud foul language. Yet he was "a child of God." "A little devil in him," was the excuse she gave to anyone who asked about him. Before she left for church she lit the candle beside the bed and knelt down to say a little prayer of hope for William Greene.

"Ah come on Ma! Ain't going to church all day enough? No, you got to carry on at home, too. Why can't you be more like Daddy? He don't do all those things you do, but he's still good, and he understands me better too. All you know is the Lord. All . . ."

"That's enough. Hush your mouth trying to be grown," was all Bea could say and they left.

Inside the church it was just like any other Sunday: the singing, shouting, and preaching. They had just got through singing a song when one of the deacons from the back tapped Bea on the shoulder. She smiled when she turned, but her smile wasn't returned.

"Why, what's wrong, brother Jones?"

"Something has happened in your home. It caught fire. The firemen came, but they came too late."

"What happened to Willy, Sadie? How's my Willy?" So many things were running through her mind. (It must have been the candle knocked to the floor by a drunken hand.) They left Bea on her knees crying and praying. And that's where Ruth found her.

"Mama, what's wrong? Mama, what's Miss Sadie doing here, Mama? Why are you crying?" Ruth kept asking. "Deacon Jones, I know something's wrong. What is it! Don't treat me like a child." Deacon Jones looked at Bea wondering whether or not to tell Ruth. Bea nodded her head, "Yes."

"Okay Ruth," he began, "I'm going to tell you."

He paused for a second. "There has been a fire at your house, and I'm afraid your father has been killed."

Ruth went into hysterics immediately. She turned and looked at her mother. "It's all your fault. You killed him with those stupid candles. You killed him, and I hate you." Hatred poured out of her eyes. The surrounding deacons restrained Ruth and took her out of the room.

Bea had taken ill, but she hadn't told anyone about her illness. One day, as Phil and Sadie were talking about something in the paper, Bea turned the page and saw Ruth's picture next to Michael's announcing they had just gotten married. Sadie wanted to kick herself for letting Bea see it. It really upset Bea. After that day, Bea never laughed. She had nightmares in the night and went into a state of depression during the day. The doctor said that her condition was serious and that you could not expect an early cure.

"Sit down Sadie," she said in such a low weak voice that Sadie had to kneel next to her bed. "I know I'm gonna die soon."

"Don't you talk like that, Bea Greene. Don't you have no more faith in God?" The sight of what used to be a big healthy, warm-hearted woman was pitiful. It brought tears to Sadie's eyes.

"Don't cry Sadie, it's for the best. I'm ready to go home to the Lord."

"Don't die, Bea, please don't die." Sadie was trying her best, because she knew that only Bea could restore her own life. If Bea had the desire, she could hold on and maybe get well. "I'll get Ruth for you, Bea."

"You talking crazy, Sadie. You know Ruth won't come here. She hates me. Don't say you'll get her cause you can't."

"Yes I can. If you just hold on, Bea, I promise I'll get her here. You would like that wouldn't you?"

"Okay," Bea said, for Sadie's sake.

The next morning Sadie asked Phil to find out where Ruth was and then to let her know. It didn't take long for Phil to find out. She was staying at the Americana Hotel in New York. Sadie immediately wrote a letter to Ruth.

The mail arrived Tuesday in New York. Ruth immediately opened the letter out of curiosity. It read:

> I'm writing because of your mama, Ruth. She's so sick. The doctor said she ain't got too long to live, Ruth, and she needs you right now. She just loves you so.

Ruth showed no sign of concern. She saw Sadie in her mind's eye. Sadie seemed to be begging her.

> —so I was wondering if you could come back to Chicago and try to cheer her up a bit before she dies. I'm telling the truth. Your father was a no-good bum. He didn't deserve your mother at all. She was too good for him. Rotten to the core he was. With all the liquor and women he used to run around with. You little fool. He didn't love you. He loved no one but himself. Your mother knew all about him: the gambling, everything. She just kept it away from you because you loved him so. He used to treat your mother bad, but she took care of him. She overlooked all the evil things he did, and she would never permit him to act bad around you. Your mother was always protecting you; that's why she never told you—even after he was killed. She loves you. More 'n anything in this world, and you won't even visit her on her deathbed. You'll turn out to be no good, Ruth. Just like your Daddy.

As she finished reading the letter, the telephone rang. Upon answering, an unfamiliar voice spoke to her, "Hello, Mrs. Jones?"

"This is Sergeant Riley from the twenty-third precinct. We have your husband down here. He's been pretty badly beaten. I suggest you call a lawyer and come down here right away."

Ruth hung up the phone and called the lawyer right away. They met at the station house and everything was settled. Michael's personal belongings were returned to him and they left. Upon reaching the apartment, Ruth repeated, "Michael, why were you arrested?"

"Listen baby, I ain't got no time to waste explaining things to you." He began to change his clothes.

"Michael, I want to know why you were put in jail. What were you doing?"

"Listen woman. Leave me alone. Just sit down and shut up." He removed a gun from the bureau and headed for the door. She tried to stop him but was smacked aside. She pulled herself together and followed him.

Following him in a cab, she noticed that Michael got out of his car on the West side of Manhattan. Women dashed toward him from all corners like mice scurrying for cheese. They talked for a while. Then Michael held out his hand to pocket their money. Ruth suffered from a twinge of regret. My God, what had she been doing to her mother after all these years? Now it was too late. Her mother was dying. She realized that what Sadie had written was true—all true. She would go to her mother right away, if it weren't already too late. She began to cry softly.

At the hospital, it was Sadie who let Ruth in.

"Oh my baby." Bea's anguish made Ruth cry.

"Mama, don't die. Please don't die. I love you so."

"Don't worry baby. I know you love me; but I'm going home. Lord knows, I'm ready to come on home. He's waiting for me, Ruth, and I'm ready to go. I love you, too." And Bea closed her eyes.

"Mama, mama, please." Ruth became hysterical. She resolved to make it up to her mother. Her life would be different.

*Terri Hughes*
*New York, New York*

## WHAT'S WRONG?

What's wrong, he says,
"Don't you believe in me anymore?"
"Have you lost faith in me?"
That old familiar line that I've heard too many times?
Belief in *him*? Faith in *him*? (he is always the focus)
Belief, Faith—it all sounds like
religion to me.
And yes, there is something wrong.
He is not going to be my religion any longer.
    I do not need a religion.
    I don't.

*Reiko Obata*
*San Diego, California*

# FISH-WIFE AND THE LITTLE GOD

Out of the tub.
Like a fish flopping
off the water
as the day tornadoes
down the drain
noisily; as all days do.

She salts herself with talcum,
dresses in a leaf green
and plops between the
bread white sheets.

He comes home hungry
enough for a horse,
but there is only woman
whom he gluttonously
swallows, making do.
He belches, full, then sleeps
dreaming he is God.
(Little does he realize
gods will die, too.)

*Mary Yeager*
*Indianapolis, Indiana*

# THE HOUSEWIFE

The house is clean
but
your mind rots,
Something's in there
aching to come out,
But it's not used to the open air—
Yes, and now the lion comes in and
roars his troubles onto you—
But you can't express yours—
not even in a
simple
meow—
And he eats your dinner
and your body too;
So you pour out the boiling wax
from your mind . . .
Was he listening?
His face lights up
and
he opens his mouth—
Oh god, he heard.
"Honey, the baby's crying."

*Shoshana Volkas*
*Claremont, California*

# CONCRETE COFFEE

"Babe,
would you
pour me
another
cup of
coffee . . .
would you
or
is that
asking
too much?"

"Would you
kindly
step down
from your
masculine
mountain
of pride
or
is that
asking
too much?"

"Is there
something
wrong, babe?"

"Yea,
i'm a
woman."

*Kristie Ogren*
*Torrance, California*

# OLD MRS. MILLER

There's a lady I see sometimes:
Old Mrs. Miller, who's lived 'round here
    for as long as anyone can remember
        the lady used to be merry
        the lady used to be pretty,
                and smiling,
                and energetic.

I wonder if it's the same person:
My lady wears wrinkles and frowns.
Maybe they're from her four young children,
                cold water flat,
                and wandering husband.

Old Mrs. Miller says I'm pretty,
                and merry,
                and smiling,
                and energetic.
And that frightens me.

*Flaurie Imberman*
*Staten Island, New York*

# CHOICE OF JOBS

I got this job about four months ago. It was a hassle, for you see, my husband and I don't see eye to eye on Women's Liberation. I found this out the hard way.

I can still hear Nancy's persistent voice, "Don't you want to be an individual? Do you mean to tell me that you actually enjoy being treated like a maid and nurse?"

"I'm not a maid or a nurse. I'm a wife and mother, Nancy. I'm not going to that Women's Lib meeting and that's final." Nancy continued to insist, so I finally decided I'd go and get her off my back.

After the meeting, I arrived at the apartment to find Mike anxiously waiting for me. "Where have you been," he snapped.

"To a meeting."

"A meeting, what kind of meeting?"

"A Women's Lib meeting."

"A what?"

"A Women's Lib meeting," I shouted.

"Women's Lib!"

I can still see the look on his face. He looked as though I had just pointed a gun at him. "You don't need to look so shocked. I just thought I'd go. I was sort of curious and I decided to keep Nancy company."

"Nancy doesn't need your company that badly. You have kids to take care of, remember?"

"You don't mean you're mad 'cause I took one afternoon off? I'm chained to this house twenty-four hours a day. I take one afternoon for myself and you get all upset."

"I'm not upset and I do realize that this house and the kids are a big job. It's just this Women's Lib garbage!"

"Typical male attitude. He goes out whenever he wants, and I take one afternoon off and he gets upset."

The next day, I got the newspaper and looked for a job that I might be interested in. After all, I was a pretty good secretary before I got married. Mike hadn't allowed me to work after the kids came. I found several that interested me, so I got dressed and went to see about them. I came home depressed. I just knew I hadn't made any impressions on the employers, but I was wrong. The next day Mr. Wilson of the ABC Co. called and asked if I could work that following Monday. My neighbor agreed to stay with the kids, so I was all set. Now, I'd have to face Mike—the hardest job of all.

When Mike came home that night, I told him. "Are you crazy; what about the kids?"

"Mrs. Williams said she'd take care of them."

"That's not the point. It's your job to take care of our children. She can't give them the love and care that you can."

"Mike, give me a chance. Please don't fight me."

"Absolutely not. I don't care to discuss it any further." He stormed out of the room.

Weeks and months passed, but Mike had not changed his attitude. Then, two months ago, I came home after a very exhausting day to find Mike sitting in front of the T.V. set. "Where have you been? I'm hungry."

"I'm sorry; I had to stay overtime."

"What's for dinner?"

"I'll let you know as soon as I make up my mind. Now please, stop rushing me."

"Now listen Linda. Let me tell you something. It was your idea to get this job. If you're gonna work overtime, that's your affair. I just want my dinner." I didn't argue with him. I gave him his dinner and went to bed. From then on, things went downhill.

Mike met me at the door of the apartment, grumbling about the fact that he needed clean shirts. That did it. "Mike, if you want clean shirts, wash them. I've got a lot to do. Just stick them in the washing machine."

"Look Linda. You're my wife. It's your job to wash them."

"My job? My job ends at 5:00," I yelled. "From now on it's up to both of us to make sure the clothes are clean and the house is in fit shape."

"Up to the two of us if you decide that you want to work? That's up to you; and you figure out how to handle both your job and your home!"

"Mike, you're being unfair. It's not as though you can't do it. You're no longer a child. I don't have to diaper and feed you your bottle." I expected to see steam coming out of his ears any moment.

"I do my part. I bring home the paycheck that pays the bills, you know."

"All right, so my pay check doesn't measure up to yours, but at least my job is more exciting than washing diapers." I took the kids and went to see my mother. Mike and I discussed it when we got back.

"Linda, I thought about what you said. You're right. I'm being pigheaded. Go right on working."

"Mike, I knew you'd see it my way. Thank you."

Mike's attitude changed. He realized that I needed a change of pace from housework. He helped me in every way that he could from then on. I came home two weeks ago to find that he had straightened up the house and he had cooked dinner. It was then that I made up my mind to quit. "Mike, I've decided to quit my job. I just wanted a chance to prove that I was doing something useful, and you've been very helpful."

"You were right, Linda. I was being silly."

"No you had your reasons, and you were right. Now my major job is to take care of the children."

Next week I start evening courses at college. Maybe when the kids are older, I'll go back to work.

*Sonia Sontiago*
*New York, New York*

# DIARY OF A TEENAGE BRIDE

Although I believe in some women's rights, I never considered myself a liberated woman. One day, when we were having a discussion on Women's Liberation in my English class, I spoke of my marriage and I realized that maybe I really was liberated.

When I was married, I was sixteen years old. I decided to play the role of a wife according to what I had heard. We got our own apartment, and we were very enthusiastic about our new life and the new roles we would be playing. I used to cook, wash dishes, clean the house, wash the clothes and iron them. At first, I found this wonderful, as I had new responsibilities and I was happy with them. But as weeks went by, I found myself more tired and less enthusiastic about the role of wife; I was beginning to feel I was Cinderella but the Prince hadn't arrived.

So, I started arguing with my husband because I didn't find it fair that I had to do all the work in the house while he sat around watching television. I decided then and there that something had to be done or our marriage would become a disaster, so I stopped doing the chores and started leaving the house in a complete mess. Of course, the arguing then got worse, until our marriage began falling apart. I knew then that if neither of us compromised, our marriage would no longer exist. Finally, my husband and I sat down calmly and had a long serious talk which resulted in a compromise. Now we help each other with the chores and we both have more time for relaxation.

So, you see, that is how I know that I'm a liberated woman because sharing is one of the most important privileges of a man or a woman.

*Rosario Rivera*
*New York, New York*

# CONTEST

A blow to the male
As she scores
With another backhand

Fuzzy gray ball
Lost in the combat
Between the sexes

*Randy Mott*
*Skaneateles, New York*

# THE EVOLUTION OF THE SEED MAN

Starting from the infinitesimal,
in a warm, black womb.
Man,

Nurtured, sheltered, formed,
waiting for his birthday.
Born.

Growing, he spreads his being out,
like tree branches, to know his world.
Embracing.

Growing, he infects everything,
like a fungus, bacterium or virus.
Poisoning.

Ageing to the shriveled, wrinkled state,
becoming smaller and smaller.
Again.

He dies, his being returns to
Its first form, the minute seed.
Changed.

The seed is blown across the skies,
now it is the nucleus of his past existence.
Reason.

Man will journey to his new beginning,
to the universal womb.

*Linda Heisen*
*Torrance, California*

# A PLEA

Kicking, crushing
hope-dreams
brutal, harsh then

striking, lashing
women.
Such a man.

Tell me what
a man
is like (you know

I've always wished
to be
one). So tell me

of the glory
of pain
the inflicted

ruination,
defeat.
My sadist, my

love, wound me with
your words.
Pierce each pore

sharply, neatly.
Ready
me for more, love.

*Mary Yeager*
*Indianapolis, Indiana*

## FOR A MAN

you have motherhood like a star shining on your forehead
the little Ingrid lies in your arms
you have learned the delicate art of feeding a child
while leading a meeting
Ingrid sucks noisily and happily at her bottle
you talk of the Movement and rub her arm
she kicks her feet and you hold her still
when she looks up, you croon to her
then you pick up the thread of the revolution—
you can feed a child well, for a man.

*Anne Fullerton*
*Paris, France*

## TENDERLY

Two teenagers fighting
A healthy fight.
"It shows their virility."
Tenderly one boy feels his bruises.

Two B-52 bomber pilots
embracing after a "good" mission.
"Comradeship."
Tenderly the victims of their bombs die.

Two baby boys sleep
arm in arm.
They've awakened;
Tenderly they cry for what they do not know.

*Stephanie Jacqueney*
*Long Beach, New York*

# HOW DIVINE A THING

> Thou, while thy babes around thee cling,
> Shalt show us how divine a thing
> A woman may be made.
>
> —*Wordsworth*

The weekly Council was drawing to a close. It had been a long and tiring session.

"Has anyone any further business to consider? If so, let her speak," the Granddam said.

After a short silence, the Matriarch of Amans spoke. "Granddam, perhaps it is time for the Council to discuss the growing restlessness of the me-krahns."

The Granddam gave a short derisive laugh. "I think not!" she said. "The me-krahns are not capable of being elsewhere than they are, and most of them know it. What do they want, a seat on the Council?" At this outrageous idea, the whole Council laughed. "No, good Matriarch," the Granddam continued, "a me-krahn's place is in the home. They are happiest there. The very few who appear discontent are no problem to us. What threat could a me-krahn pose to a council of krahns? We will perhaps consider the me-krahn issue another day. The Council of Matriarchs is dismissed."

The Granddam was relaxing in her private chambers, a glass of brandy in her hand. Near her sat one of her oldest and most trusted friends, Soror Libera, who had a reputation as one of the foremost psychiatrists in the nation. Momentarily away from the pressures and tensions of her office, the Granddam found her mind wandering to the issue of the me-krahns.

"Tell me, Soror," she said. "What do you think about the restlessness of a few of the me-krahns?"

"Personally or professionally?"

"Both."

"Probably the result of a glandular disorder," Soror Libera answered.

"Is that all?" the Granddam asked.

"Well," Soror Libera began, "it has, of course, been proven that me-krahns suffer from childhood from varying degrees of womb-envy. When they realize that they don't have the ability to bring forth life, as krahns can (with a minimal amount of help from the me-krahns, of course), they naturally feel inadequate."

"Yes," said the Granddam, "but we help them to release this frustration, in a socially acceptable way, by the yearly games."

"This does help, of course," Soror Libera conceded. "The me-krahns have certain primitive aggressive drives, happily absent in krahns, and the yearly games give them a therapeutic opportunity to release them. They cannot help themselves, of course; medically speaking, their primitive drives are the result of a hormone imbalance inherent in their sex. It is for this very reason that we cannot allow them a seat in government—their primitive drives, their tendency toward aggression when uncontrolled, makes them too unstable. And up to now, all me-krahns have been perfectly content."

"And why shouldn't they be?" interjected the Granddam. "We take care of them, we shield them from the worries of providing for a family. We marry them, we adore them, we entrust them with the care of our most precious commodity, our children. I'm sure if I were a me-krahn, I would be very happy."

"Yes, Granddam. The me-krahns as a sex have every reason to be content. They will not allow the inane clamorings of a few sexually-frustrated, neurotic me-krahns to disturb their happiness. It is obvious to anyone that they are the favored, protected sex.

"And besides," Soror Libera continued, "speaking frankly, there are certain things they simply do not have the capability of doing. Can you imagine trusting a me-drahn to defend you in court? Or to invest your money? Or serve on the Council?! It is preposterous. Me-krahns just don't have the ability—after all, look who has ended up running things."

"You are quite right," the Granddam said. "You have put things into perspective again. We must do our best to help the me-krahns accept their inadequacies, and become useful, fulfilled beings in spite of them."

Soror Libera nodded in assent.

"But, come, friend," the Granddam continued. "Enough talk of minor matters of state. Let us talk of more interesting, important things. I have approved the next appropriation—costly, but necessary—to the researchers working on the Rahlston Hypothesis for a completely safe, painless procedure for childbirth . . . ."

*Lynn Bottum*
*Ann Arbor, Michigan*

# THE OTHER NIGHT

When Daddy came home the other night, he was singing. I sat in my room and I hung out the window, combing my hair as he sat whistling on the porch swing. The swing creaked under his heavy body. He swatted the mosquitoes and the flies away with those big beefy hands of his.

"Daddy," I called down to him. "Why don't you come inside now. You've got work tomorrow."

"Oh work," he said. "A man's locked in like a goddamned dog, goddamned dog. How's a man supposed to live when thinking only of his bread? As far as I can see, work can go straight to hell and back again. The night's not done with yet. You go back on into bed. I've got thinking to do."

I closed the window and slipped back into bed. He was singing again.

"Daddy," I called down again. "Daddy, Mommy's waiting for you and you're keeping the neighbors awake with that singing of yours. Daddy, why don't you come on inside now. I can't sleep with you out there."

"Get yourself back to bed and hold your tongue. That's a fine thing, a fine thing to be sure: a daughter telling her old dad what to do and how to do it. I work hard for your food, little lady, and I won't have you taking liberties with your tongue."

"Yes, Daddy."

I was awake before the sun hit my bed, maybe an hour before. Daddy was still sitting on the porch swing. His face was grey and his body heaved with every breath he took. I put on some clothes and went downstairs.

"Daddy," I said. "It's morning. Wake up now and go fix yourself up, wash and shave."

He moaned a bit and I said, "Change your clothes too, Daddy. You've pissed in your pants."

He looked up with his grey eyes, now red rimmed and swollen.

"That's a fine thing for a girl to be saying to her dad. Get on and fix me up some coffee or something. I'll be doing the ordering around here from now on. Fine thing, a daughter ordering her father about."

I went inside and as the door slammed behind me, Mommy called to me from her room.

"Is your daddy home yet?"

"No Mommy. I mean, yes."

"It's about time. I thought for sure he was dead by now."

"He's been home for a while now."

"Where was he then? I didn't hear him come in."

"On the porch. Let him be, Mommy. He's so tired."

"I should say he'd be tired, out all night. I'll let him be. What would I want with him? One of the ugliest men in the county. Don't you never ever ask me why I married him. It'd make me blush and you blush too."

I went upstairs and combed my hair for a while. I was tired and I hung out the window, watching the men with their lunch pails pass by my dad and say hey and good morning to him. Daddy's eyes were shut and he ran his thick fingers through his hair, where no other hands seemed to want to travel and it made me feel bad for my dad. I had always thought he was a handsome man.

The sun rose higher and higher until it hung way above the hills. The town looked grey, as grey as the coal dust it sprang from. I put down my comb and went to shake my daddy awake.

*Jennifer Crichton*
*New York, New York*

## CRYSTALLIZED CONFORMITY

The way people say.
That's how to do it.
Chained by the minds of a smoldering few,
  dampened and harnessed to become those few.
They constantly inflict with their bounds,
Because their bounds are their freedom
  (or knowledge of freedom).
They can't capture me. At least not yet.
I'm not ready to be confined by a cell.
I need to move.
    To dream.
    To be.
They don't.

*Valerie Rosenquist*
*Crown Point, New York*

# POEM

The poem starts with a long moan.
everybody runs for cover.

I finally speak sensibly
. . . . . to empty trees . . . . .
"let's make up our minds now.
Motives—listed as such:
1) Simply a platonic relationship.
2) We all love a good time
a good [- - - -]
a good laugh.
3) Smash our skulls together and make
a big emotional mess on the rug,
groove on the colors for a couple days.
4) Pretend we're in love, and while nobody's
looking try to convince ourselves."

Carry me to the highest cliff,
and drop me off the limestone overhang.
I'll listen to your love songs
all the way to the pine
–crash–
birch
–crash–
rock
–crash–
wa
ter

*Windy Wilson*
*Ann Arbor, Michigan*

## REHABILITATION

When my mind
says 'NO,"
but my body yields
to your
confident caresses,
I know it's time
for a new type
of brainwash.

*Flaurie Imberman*
*New York, New York*

## THERE IT SITS

there it sits
tall and
mighty
swelling her finger
with chartreuse yarn
a symbol of
love
possession
security
with it
she feels satisfied
she's someone
of
importance
never
will she take
it off
even
for him (he doesn't count.)

*Laurie B. Lommen*
*Buxton, North Dakota*

# DEAR J.

Dear J.
What I was talking about
    was the pain and sorrow
        of being a sister
            today and tomorrow,
and as your face contorted
into a smile, then laughter
at each sexist phrase I repeated
the pain grew into anger.
[- - - -] you, my sister,
[- - - -] you for condoning our oppression
with your giggles.
[- - - -] you, my sister,
[- - - -] you for supporting our oppressor
in his laughter.
The struggling woman lawyer
is you, my sister.
The secretary sex kitten
is also you, my sister.
Every sexist phrase I parroted
is deeply engraved in the experience of being
    "a real woman"
Sister J.,
you can be anything you want to be
    "a real woman" OR "a chick."
Dear J.
What I was talking about
    was the pain and sorrow
        of being yourself
            today and tomorrow.

*Anne Fullerton*
*Paris, France*

# THE WONDERFUL STORY OF RITA ACKERMAN

When Rita Ackerman was eighteen, she wasn't married. Neither were any of her friends. They thought Rita was typical. Only weird people were married when they were eighteen.

When Rita Ackerman was twenty-two, she still wasn't married. Some of her friends were married or at least engaged. They had met Mr. Right in college, but not Rita. She had met plenty of misters but not Mr. Right.

When Rita Ackerman was twenty-five, she wasn't married yet, as her friends would say. Most of them were married and some even had kids. Rita was free. She had plenty of men but no husbands. Her friends no longer thought she was typical. They thought she was weird.

When Rita Ackerman was twenty-nine, she still remained single. Some of her friends were already on their second husband, and most of them had kids. They'd all invite her over to have whiskey sours with some eligible man from work. Eligible men turned Rita off. She liked men, but had no desire to have a husband. Several friends suggested a psychiatrist. She suggested the same for them.

Rita was now a thirty-two year old bachelorette and likely to remain so. In the past three years, her friends had convinced her this was crazy. She joined the Swinging Singles and had a miserable time. She only dated eligible men. It was difficult to find someone over thirty and eligible; but her friends managed; so did her students.

She was a teacher, which made things worse: an old maid school marm, uch! She couldn't help it that she wanted to be free and not have children or dogs or husbands to put up with. She wasn't odd or weird. She was just different.

Her friends didn't think this difference was so nice, and Rita was starting to agree. She'd tell the girls in her homeroom about the Swinging Singles Weekend in the Berkshires and they'd all cheer her on. Even the sixteen year olds thought she was crazy.

Rita decided to end it all. She couldn't stand the harassment, so she went to visit her brother in New Rochelle. There she met Larry Tonken.

When Larry Tonken was eighteen, he wasn't married; when Larry Tonken was twenty-two, he still wasn't married; when Larry Tonken was twenty-five, he wasn't married yet as his friends would say; when Larry Tonken was twenty-nine, he still remained single. Larry was now a thirty-five year old bachelor and likely to remain so. Everyone convinced him he was crazy. He liked women, but he hated wives. He was perfect for Rita—or so thought her sister-in-law.

Rita thought he was pretty neat too. He had never been eligible, but she hadn't been eligible either. It was just great. Their relationship was perfect, but everyone around them started talking about marriage. God, it was awful.

Soon even Rita and Larry were convinced it was the only thing to do. On Christmas day, Larry gave Rita THE ring. Everyone was so proud of Rita. She had finally caught her man.

She had not of course. They weren't planning on getting married, just on getting engaged. It would shut everyone up. So Rita and Larry remained fiancees for the next seventeen months. After that, people began asking questions. It was getting Larry and Rita sick. They loved each other, but they couldn't imagine getting married; an engagement was bad enough. Everyone was sure they were mad.

The engagement was finally broken. It was such a happy occasion, at least for Larry and Rita. All of their friends cried. Rita could handle them. They were old enough to understand that husbands and wives do get a little sickening now and then. But what would she tell her homeroom?

There was one way in which Rita was weird. She wanted her girls, as she called them, to respect her. How could they respect an unengaged woman? She was miserable.

She used to enjoy having little conferences with the girls, showing them how to catch a man. Rita was an expert at catching men; she just didn't like to keep them. She was sure the girls would no longer listen to her. "Maybe they won't notice the ring is gone," she thought. That was absurd. They were the first to notice it was there; they'd certainly notice it was gone.

She couldn't sleep that night, facing her homeroom troubled her so. Rita was so mixed up. After thirty-three years of remaining unattached she hadn't yet realised it was the only way for her.

The next morning, she tip-toed into her homeroom and folded her hands behind her back, so as not to look suspicious. No one had noticed the ring was gone, until suddenly the fateful announcement sounded, "Please stand and join me in the pledge of allegiance to our flag."

She placed her hand across her chest. One of the girls shouted, "Your ring, your ring, it's gone."

With tears in her eyes and determination in her voice, Rita answered, "I shall no longer lie. I don't want to get married and I never have. Men are wonderful, but husbands I can do without. You can live as you choose, but I shall remain single."

A hush fell over the room, when suddenly a girl in the back screamed, "Yeah Miss Ackerman! We knew you were on our side all along." The whole class rose despite the pledge of allegiance, and gave Rita Ackerman the standing ovation she deserved.

*Susan Merkert*
*Eggertsville, New York*

# A WOMAN'S ANSWER TO RUDYARD KIPLING

There is a time, a single moment, even in our complex society, when childhood ends and adulthood begins. Sometimes it is marked by great ceremony and ritual. More often, it is one small, private act, one unhonored and unnoticed deed, when a child knows he is a child no more.

For me, it was the day I bought my own sanitary napkins. On many previous occasions, I'd given the task to my mother, but the time had come for me to face this trial alone.

I felt pretty good that day. The sun was shining, and my heart was light. I got off the bus and walked nonchalantly across the parking lot to the drugstore. For a moment I felt fear, but I gritted my teeth and pushed the door open. The thousands of rows of shelves stunned me with their garish plastic repetition. I walked quickly through the giant store to a back corner.

Shelf upon shelf of bulky pastel boxes greeted my eyes, all attempting or claiming to look discreet, and being about as convincing as an eight year old child in blue pajamas with "Superman" printed across the front. I checked my wallet and began making my selections from the convocation amassed before me.

A small sign, taped to the shelf, declared (again, discreetly) "ALL CONTRACEPTIVE FOAMS SOLD ONLY AT DRUG COUNTER." Hmmmmm. Someday, I'll have THAT trauma. I can see it now.

"Um, er, uh, that is, uh, my um, er, uh, my uh, MOM wants some, uh, mumble, sputter, mumble."

"How old are you, kid?"

"Uh, thirty-six. I'm short for my age . . . ."—but back to the immediate.

A man looks down the aisle, blushes, and walks away. This would be a good place to come to read. No interruptions. I guess the floor is radioactive in this part of the store.

I picked a box, walked to the checkout. The cashier looked at me sympathetically, much as one regards a leper. They slipped it in a brown paper bag, for a final touch of discretion. I left the store.

Home, I leaned against the stairs, tired but successful. In the background, Michael Jackson sang "Ben."

I'd done it.

Today, I was a man!

*Laurie A. Walker*
*Syracuse, New York*

## SHE WHO STOOPS TO CONQUER

She who stoops to conquer
Will find that once she's down,
It's not easy to stand straight again.
A Woman never stoops to conquer.
A Woman never stoops.
A Woman will break before she'll bend.
After all, Mr. Goldsmith, how can you be
In two places at once, when you're really
Nowhere at all?

*Joan Irene Wieleba*
*Wetherfield, Connecticut*

## THE PEDESTAL

You
Who have placed me
Up here . . . . .
Please
        let
            me
                down.
Please.
Theairistight,
Theairistight.

I can no longer breathe.

*Flaurie Imberman*
*New York, New York*

# I SIT ALONE

i sit alone
and wait
for someone
who may never
come

but yet
i sit alone
and wait for someone
who may never
come

yet
i sit alone
and wait
and wait
wait
wait

*Laurie B. Lommen*
*Buxton, North Dakota*

## SONG 16

I want to forget I am a woman
crammed into a mold of makeup
every morning,
squeezed into a miniskirt I worry about
every time I sit,
my legs covered in stockings
that catch on
every snag,
being propositioned on
every street,
always being stared at by
every body,
always being put down by
every man.

I want to wear jeans today
I don't have to play games that way.
I want to be looked to for my brain
not my breasts,
not my legs,
I want to be kept from going insane
as we do
when left
with nothing, with no one to say
You are somebody,
not Some Body
a shallow, commercial view of self
a sour self-deprecating laugh
we swim back in our sea
of menstrual fluids and scented creams
every night.

*Anne Fullerton*
*Paris, France*

# PRETENDING

Don't ask me
for a ride home
or to talk
with you at your locker
I'm so tired of seeing you now
yet I want to get closer.
To feel your eyes
and go inside you
No, don't touch me
I pretend I've got to go
to my next class
And you pull away also
I never even touched you
but why I can't break away
  I'll never know . . .
Someday I'm going to say
that we can't go on like we do
The games we play, the roles
  it's really not me
that you see
I'm a totally different person (I wish)
But really you'll never understand me
and I'll surely never understand you
So maybe it's better
  for us
to be separate
instead of spending our energies
on trying to be one (won).

*Reiko Obata*
*San Diego, California*

# POEM

the moon shadows don't mend right
with a lover lying easy in a field . . . .
. . . . . he has . . . no . . . . face . . . .
The weeds haven't eyes
so never mind, unless the mice hear,
no one will.
Sleep, lady, until the
morning vanishes this
midnight game of hide 'n seek . . .
'cause everybody's hiding . . . . . . .
and nobody's counting . . . .
Keep the stillness near the quiet
until the sun leans over and
calls . . . . . .

Alll-eee—alll-eee—all-come-freeeee

and the dew rises.

*Windy Wilson*
*Ann Arbor, Michigan*

# VARSITY SPORTS—1984

It is the year 1984 and our Varsity Basketball team has just won the State Championship. The girls were just wonderful and held out with no trouble at all. The day would have been a complete success had the boys not interrupted the half time activities to gripe about their sport's program. They held up signs with slogans such as, "Equality for Males" and "Discrimination." For as long as one can remember, the girls have dominated sports and have been physically capable of handling them. All of a sudden in the last year, the skinny boys decided that they wanted a complete functional sports program such as the girls have.

The girls have a very complex program where every sport possible is played. There are Varsity and J.V. teams with a very complete intramural program. The best possible coaches are hired at very attractive prices and the state is very free with money. The boys, though, have a very nice after-school intramural setup and one of the school's music teachers is more than willing to help them.

Anyway, the boys have become obsessed with the idea of restructuring their sports program. They made a list of what they wanted and took it to the Board of Education.

It is agreed that boys are not serious enough to accept the responsibility of Varsity or J.V. sports. Last year when Alan Witty tried out for baseball, he missed practice twice while chasing his girlfriend around. (She is on Varsity track.) Since the boys have been lacking physical training since they were born, they tend to be very skinny and fragile. Very few boys can withstand any physical contact at all. They are really scared and concerned about hurting or scarring their soft bodies. None of the male teachers want to coach boys' sports, because they feel they are underpaid compared to the women coaches. In reply to this, all one can say is that it takes time to build a program and one must start at the bottom.

I must also add that the girls have a point when it comes to space. They were involved first in sports, so therefore, they should have priority over all equipment and space. The girls bring in hundreds and hundreds of dollars from their sports events so they should get the first say on what times and rooms they need for practice. To think the boys who don't contribute anything complain about this is just unbelievable. Seriously, who would consider paying money to see sissy boys playing basketball?

The boys would not give in, though, so eventually the Board of Education, along with the women coaches, decided on a compromise. The boys would have a Varsity sports program and after awhile, games could be set up with other schools. Of course these games will be scheduled around the girls' games and will be free because no one will pay to watch them. If you are looking at this objectively we really have not given them much, but, in my opinion, it is more than they deserve.

*Lynn Warshaw*
*Ann Arbor, Michigan*

# ONCE UPON A TIME

Once upon a time, there were six young maidens. They were all radiantly beautiful, innocent and virtuous. Each maiden has her own unique story, which every well-taught child and adult should know by heart. None of the six radiantly beautiful, innocent and virtuous maidens knew one another during the height of their collective radiant beauty, innocence, and virtue—that part of their story with which we are all familiar. But they met years afterwards—years beyond where story tellers left them—when their lives were no longer fairy tales.

The first maiden's name, surprisingly enough, was Beauty, and she was the most beautiful maiden they had ever seen, said all who set eyes upon her. She was extremely virtuous and had two wicked sisters, who really helped set off her virtue. She had a father who loved her very much. One day her father went travelling and got into hot water with a beast for picking a rose for Beauty from his garden. As punishment, he had to give up his daughter or his own life. He was loathe to give up Beauty, but she insisted on meeting the Beast. Perhaps she, too, had heard the rumor that he was very wealthy. The Beast was very hairy and had acne. But he had a heart of gold, and fell in love with Beauty immediately, which wasn't surprising—he was only human. Beauty consented to marry the Beast, and he was so overjoyed that someone was willing to marry one as ugly as himself that, when Beauty kissed him, he turned into a prince, which, at the time, she thought very fortunate.

The next beautiful maiden was named Cinderella. She and Beauty had a lot in common, because they both had wicked sisters to set off their virtue; however, Cinderella didn't know that she had a partner in misery, so she spent most of her time in front of the fireplace, which was how she got her name. One day, the King and Queen gave a ball for their son, who was called the Prince. All the young debutantes were invited. Cinderella's sisters wouldn't let her go to the ball, and left her alone, telling her to clean the fireplace—which was clean already, since Cinderella hated dirty bed linens, and all other dirt.

However, Cinderella did get to the ball, by contrivances known only too well, and when she arrived, dressed like a princess, all who set eyes on her said that she was the most beautiful maiden they had ever seen. (Including the Prince.) After this primary seduction, and a lot of luck, the Prince and Cinderella found each other and were married.

The third maiden was Aurora, The Dawn, and she was a Princess. All who set eyes on her said that she was the most beautiful maiden they had ever seen. However, she had a curse laid on her, and on her sixteenth birthday, an evil old woman slipped three tranquilizers into her coffee in a restaurant when she wasn't looking. After drinking the entire cup, she passed out on the restaurant floor; she went into a very long coma. Her parents and friends were struck dumb with horror and ceased to function. The doctors did all they could. Finally, a charming, young, handsome intern decided to try something different. He went into Aurora's room, where she lay asleep, and falling in love with her instantly, he kissed her on the mouth, whereupon she awoke and they were married.

The fourth maiden, Snow White, was a Southern belle. She lived on a big plantation with her father, who was King, and her evil, beautiful stepmother, who owned a magic mirror, which is probably more famous than Snow White herself. All who set eyes on Snow White said that she was the most beautiful maiden they had ever seen. Snow White's stepmother was insanely jealous of her, and convinced her husband to send his daughter to a college in a big Northern city, an environment which the wicked stepmother was sure would kill Snow White, owing to her delicate constitution.

Snow White, however, thrived in her new environment, and became very popular. She took up with seven members of the Phi Shorta Fatta fraternity—keeping their rooms in order and mending their clothes, in return for their writing her term papers. She was soon elected campus queen.

Meanwhile, when the stepmother asked her mirror who was the fairest on the East Coast, the mirror answered "Snow White." She fell into a rage and flew North to poison the maiden. After several attempts, she succeeded. Snow White ate a poisoned apple and her seven friends mournfully carried her out of the frat house. A young graduate student, upon seeing Snow White's lifeless body, couldn't help claiming that he knew first aid. His mouth-to-mouth resuscitation revived her; they fell in love, and were married.

Our fifth young maiden was given up for adoption to a very old woman, who kept her locked up in a tower. The maiden's name was Rapunzel, and if people had been able to set eyes on her, they would have said she was the most beautiful maiden they had ever seen. Rapunzel had very long, golden tresses. The old woman, who was a witch, used to climb up these tresses in order to reach the room at the top of the tower, which was very badly designed, having no stairs. Eventually, Rapunzel developed a very strong scalp.

One day a prince saw the witch climb up Rapunzel's hair. When he saw the maiden, he fell in love with her immediately and decided he would try to climb up himself. He fooled Rapunzel into letting him up, and when she saw him, she fell in love with him at once. Though the prince was not very good looking, Rapunzel thought him handsome, for she had never seen a man before.

But the witch found out and was furious. She cut off the ungrateful Rapunzel's tresses and threw the maid into the wilderness to wander lost and alone. The witch tricked the Prince, who was only of average intelligence, into climbing up Rapunzel's severed locks. But when he reached the window, he realized that either Rapunzel wasn't there or that she had undergone a drastic aging process, and he jumped down fifty feet into a briar patch and blinded himself. Rapunzel and the Prince found each other, though, and the Prince had a cornea transplant so that he could see again. Then they were married.

Our last maiden was a house painter's daughter, and it must be noted that being a lower class heroine, not so much is known of her looks—though probably all who set eyes on her thought she was the most beautiful maiden they had ever seen—nor is her name recorded, so we shall refer to her as Jill.

Jill's father was constantly making her live up to impossible ideals. One day, he bragged that she could paint an eighteen room house overnight. She was brought before the King, who set her to work on one of his houses that night. Her weeping brought a little man. He said he was a social worker and would do the job for free. When the King saw the painted rooms, he gave Jill a larger house, and the same thing happened. But the third night, when Jill was given a veritable mansion to paint, the little social worker demanded Jill's firstborn child in return for the favor. She had no choice but to consent.

Jill married the King's son, and had a baby very soon afterwards. Jill was Catholic and knew that more babies would soon ensue, and therefore decided she could part with this one. It would be well cared for. But when her husband discovered what she planned to do, he was enraged. When the little social worker arrived, therefore, Jill begged him to accept some other gift. He refused, but said that if she could guess the name of the organization for which he worked, he would leave her in peace. She had nine guesses, and by very good fortune, she found out that the organization was called The Relevant Union of More Poverty and Less Equality. Her correct guess sent the social worker into a rage, and he stomped away and became a stockbroker.

The storytellers have gone away. We will pick up where they left off.

. . . ever after.

Beauty's prince was not at all what she had expected him to be. In fact, she somewhat doubted that he was a prince at all. True, he was extremely handsome. But she rather preferred the hairy, acne-covered Beast, who was so honest and understanding, to this demanding Adonis, this petulant male, this child, this husband, who claimed to be her lover metamorphosed.

Yes, Beauty had most certainly married a total stranger. The man's conceit after the Great Change was overpowering. By the time Beauty and the Prince had been married two years, the Prince had had three affairs. He was not in the least bit discreet about them, for he assumed that his wife had neither the brains to notice them nor the nerve to mention them.

Beauty, however, was not a stupid woman. Her husband underestimated her, for she was completely aware of his lascivious nature after two years, and she did have the nerve to mention it. The Prince gained some respect for his intelligent wife, and became more discreet about his affairs, which soon doubled in number.

Much of Beauty's good nature turned to bitterness. She had certainly learned the hard way that virtue did not pay. Her life and happiness were crumbling at her feet, all because she had asked for a rose instead of a ruby.

Cinderella's prince owned a chain of men's clothing stores, so he had more of a profession than Beauty's prince, who merely worked in an office, doing nothing specific.

Many people said of Cinderella that she had gone from rags to riches. This, however, was debatable. True, she no longer spent most of her time in front of the fireplace. She slept with her husband in a large canopied bed, although occasionally she yearned for her former sleeping place. But Cinderella's life was hardly glamorous. Her Prince—Prince Ashburn—couldn't help remembering that he had impulsively married a kitchen servant because she had little feet; and he couldn't help feeling a pang of regret that he hadn't made a more prudent and advantageous choice. He, therefore, often fell into imagining that he was still a wealthy bachelor with a fulltime housekeeper.

Of course, Prince Ashburn couldn't renounce full responsibility for his housekeeper, since she had borne him a child, who was now a rather spoiled boy of five. So family life was carried on calmly, united by a close servant-master relationship.

Princess Aurora's husband, the charming Dr. Marcus Prince, was now a well-practiced surgeon. He was able to secure an ample supply of tranquilizers for his wife, who was now a well practiced neurotic insomniac. She was named for the dawn, but she rarely saw it, her sleeping pills wearing off at one or two in the afternoon.

Aurora and her husband lived in a rather large suburban mansion with a lot of ground and three servants. They had two boys, aged ten and six, and an eight year old girl, and a French poodle. The oldest boy was in boarding school and the other two in fancy schools near home. They saw very little of either parent. Aurora spent most of her time in the beauty parlor or drinking in her room. Her husband was usually on call at the hospital.

Aurora was, not surprisingly, rather unaware of her surroundings. She was behind the times. The charming Dr. Marcus Prince said she acted as if she'd been asleep for a century. But she was usually oblivious to what her husband said. So her neutral and flat oblivion continued, interrupted only by an occasional fit of alcoholic anger or sober depression.

Prince Harry Denver (or "Professor," as some preferred to call him, not knowing he was a Prince) did not get the intellectual stimulation from his wife that his genius IQ demanded. After all, he had fallen in love with Snow White, the campus queen, before she had opened her mouth. By that time, it was too late—he was happily, wholeheartedly, and uncontrollably in love. It wasn't until later that he found out about the term papers and the Phi Shorta Fatta fraternity.

The fact that Snow White refused to sever the connection with her seven friends caused a lot of tension between the couple and was responsible for many a fight. Prince Harry doubted the morality of the connection and became extremely jealous. He was not only jealous of the fact that his wife did not direct her total affections toward himself, but also because he felt Snow White placed his superior intelligence below that of her friends. And this made him feel extremely awkward. He wished he had written those term papers.

Snow White and Prince Harry had two children, a boy and a girl, who were both small for their age. They were plump, rosy and well-behaved young things, and their mother loved them dearly. They became the great joy of her life, her favorite companions, for after her friends acquired their degrees, they moved away, although they wrote Snow White regularly. Prince Harry became very involved with the economics department and his intellectually stimulating associates, coming home late for dinner, often with his side-kicks in tow.

Ever since their marriage, Rapunzel's prince seemed to see her with different eyes. She didn't appear so exceedingly beautiful, and he couldn't understand why. The fact was, of course, that Rapunzel's long, golden tresses had hidden her entire face except for her big, beautiful blue eyes. It turned out that her eyes were not her only large feature—her nose was also rather prominent. Rapunzel also had another problem: split ends. Her hair simply wouldn't grow back properly. She tried everything, from Protein Twenty-one to actually writing Vidal Sassoon.

Rapunzel, too, found that she had been rather disillusioned. After seeing other men, she found Prince John Doe rather ordinary. But by that time, it was too late.

So their marriage became a rather mediocre and unexciting way of life. In fact, the only out-of-the-ordinary event that occurred within five years of marriage was the birth of twins, who were christened Joe and John, Jr.

Every day Prince John Doe went to work at eight-thrity. He returned home at five-thirty. Rapunzel kept house and took care of the twins. She had dinner ready by six. Prince John liked meat and potatoes, so that was the usual fare.

One baby followed the next for Jill and her prince. Their first child was born six months after the marriage—which is a pretty good indication of the first and foremost reason for what turned out to be a rather incompatible marriage. For while the little social worker was painting the King's house, the King's son slipped into Jill's room. He was rather drunk, and she was rather lonely, so things proceeded rather naturally from there. When the King heard the two were married—for they eloped—he disowned his son.

Now Jill's prince—Prince Jack Crown—was nearer to a pauper than a prince, so we will call him a princeling. He became foreman for a construction firm. Jack was a good father, and his seven children—acquired over a six-year time span—were very fond of him. Jack had never quite forgiven Jill for promising their first child to a social worker. He couldn't understand how she would have had the heart to part with one of their darlings.

Jill was somewhat lacking in the motherly instinct. With seven children—the oldest of whom was seven years old, the younger three still in diapers—and another one coming soon, she had no time for such nonsense. She had decided flatly that her eighth would be her last. At twenty-six, her figure was ruined, the house was a constant mess, she had help only once a week, and she was a bundle of nerves. She had been a delicate girl, and not at all cut out for this kind of life. The children were somewhat afraid of her irritability, and looked forward to their father's return each evening. Jill was a sensitive woman: Jack, somewhat lacking in understanding. He wondered why his wife seemed unhappy.

So, here we have six heroines, six paragons of femininity, with six different backgrounds, living in six different spheres of life, but leading six lives strangely similar in their lack of excitement and in their mediocrity. They met afterwards, when they had forgotten the only part we remember, or are aware of. They met afterwards and became friends, or perhaps enemies. They were neighbors or lived miles apart. Some resolved to accept their lives; some, to ignore them; some, to fight for something more. These women were all women caught in the same clever trap; and they knew one another afterwards, for they were sisters sharing the same pain.

*Ruth L. Williams*
*Bala Cynwyd, Pennsylvania*